WESTERN JOURNEYS

Western Journeys

DISCOVERING THE SECRETS OF THE LAND

D ANIEL W OOD

and

B EVERLEY S INCLAIR

RAINCOAST BOOKS

Vancouver

To those who shared their secrets

First published in 1997 by

Raincoast Books
8680 Cambie Street
Vancouver, B.C.
v6p 6m9
(604) 323-7100

10 9 8 7 6 5 4 3 2 1

CANADIAN CATALOGUING IN PUBLICATION DATA

Wood, Daniel.
Western journeys

ISBN 1-55192-069-7

1. Canada, Western – Description and travel. 2. Natural history – Canada, Western. 3. Wood, Daniel – Journeys – Canada, Western. 4. Sinclair, Beverley, 1955- – Journeys – Canada, Western. I. Sinclair, Beverley, 1955- II. Title.
FC3205.4.W66 1997   917.204'3   c96-910816-8
F1060.W66 1997

Text Design by DesignGeist
Project Editor: Michael Carroll
Copy Editor: Joanne Richardson
Map: Eric Leinberger

Printed and bound in Hong Kong

Raincoast Books gratefully acknowledges the support of the Canada Council, the Department of Canadian Heritage, and the British Columbia Arts Council.

PAGE II The Murtle River in British Columbia's Wells Gray Provincial Park assumes the quality of a dream as it flows away from 137-metre-high Helmcken Falls. D. WIGGETT/FIRST LIGHT

PAGES IV-V These aspens are now leafless; in the summer, though, their leaves will rattle distinctively in the slightest evening breeze. AL HARVEY

PAGE X Incredibly coloured bat stars, members, curiously, of the class *Stelleroidea* and the subclass *Asteroidea,* litter the intertidal zone of the Queen Charlotte Islands' Burnaby Narrows by the thousands. ART WOLFE

CONTENTS

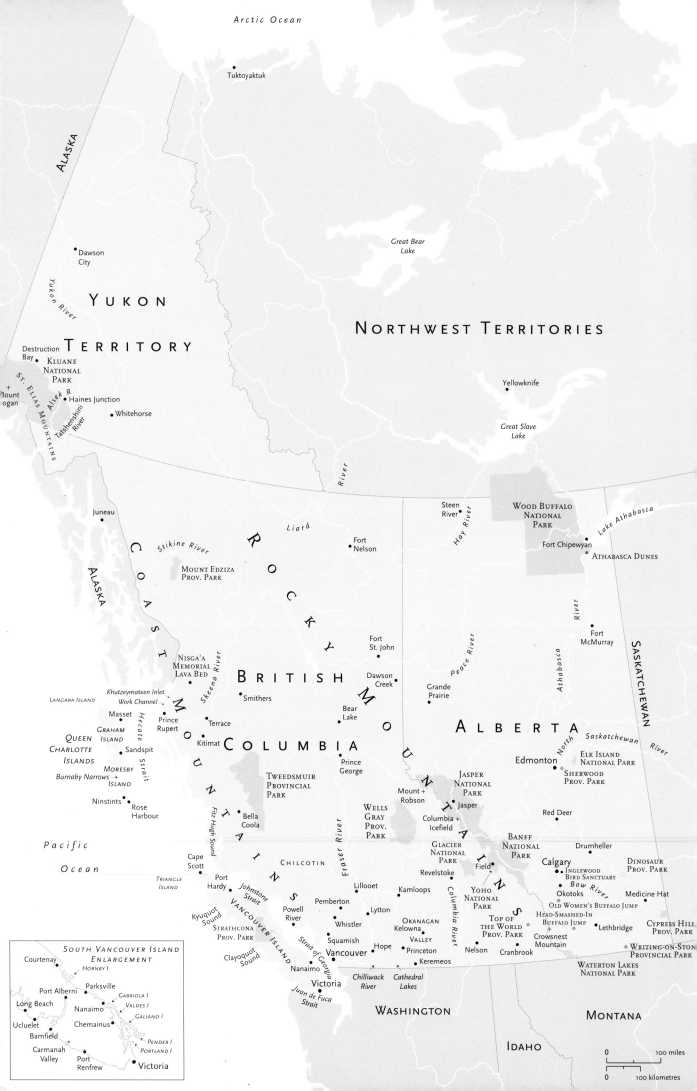

Arctic Ocean

YUKON TERRITORY

Tuktoyaktuk

Dawson City

Destruction Bay
KLUANE NATIONAL PARK

Yukon River

St. Elias Mountains
+ Mount Logan

Alsek R
Haines Junction
Tatshenshini River
Whitehorse

NORTHWEST TERRITORIES

Great Bear Lake

Yellowknife

Great Slave Lake

River

Juneau

ALASKA

COAST MOUNTAINS

Stikine River

MOUNT EDZIZA PROV. PARK

R O C K Y

Liard

Steen River

Hay River

WOOD BUFFALO NATIONAL PARK

Lake Athabasca

Fort Chipewyan
ATHABASCA DUNES

Fort Nelson

NISGA'A MEMORIAL LAVA BED

Khutzeymateen Inlet
Work Channel

Skeena River

Smithers

Fort St. John

Dawson Creek

Grande Prairie

Peace River

River

Fort McMurray

Athabasca

SASKATCHEWAN

LANGARA ISLAND

Masset

Hecate Strait

GRAHAM ISLAND

Prince Rupert

Terrace

Kitimat

Bear Lake

BRITISH COLUMBIA

M O U N T A I N S

ALBERTA

Saskatchewan River
North

Athabasca River

QUEEN CHARLOTTE ISLANDS

Sandspit

MORESBY ISLAND

Burnaby Narrows →

Ninstints

Rose Harbour

Prince George

Edmonton

ELK ISLAND NATIONAL PARK

SHERWOOD PROV. PARK

Pacific

Ocean

TRIANGLE ISLAND

Fitz Hugh Sound

Bella Coola

TWEEDSMUIR PROVINCIAL PARK

Fraser River

CHILCOTIN

WELLS GRAY PROV. PARK

Mount + Robson

JASPER NATIONAL PARK

Jasper

Columbia + Icefield

Red Deer

GLACIER NATIONAL PARK

BANFF NATIONAL PARK

Field

Drumheller

Cape Scott

Port Hardy

Johnstone Strait

Powell River

V A N C O U V E R I S L A N D

Kyuquot Sound

STRATHCONA PROV. PARK

Clayoquot Sound

Lillooet

Pemberton

Whistler

Squamish

Nanaimo

Strait of Georgia

Vancouver

Hope

Kamloops

Revelstoke

Lytton

Okanagan Kelowna

VALLEY

Columbia River

YOHO NATIONAL PARK

TOP OF THE WORLD PROV. PARK

Crowsnest Mountain

Calgary

INGLEWOOD BIRD SANCTUARY

Bow River

Okotoks

OLD WOMEN'S BUFFALO JUMP

HEAD-SMASHED-IN BUFFALO JUMP

Medicine Hat

Lethbridge

CYPRESS HILL PROV. PARK

DINOSAUR PROV. PARK

Victoria

Chilliwack River

CATHEDRAL Lakes

Princeton

Keremeos

Nelson

Cranbrook

WRITING-ON-STONE PROVINCIAL PARK

WATERTON LAKES NATIONAL PARK

Juan de Fuca Strait

WASHINGTON

MONTANA

IDAHO

SOUTH VANCOUVER ISLAND ENLARGEMENT

Courtenay

Hornby I

Parksville

Port Alberni

Gabriola I

Long Beach

Nanaimo

Valdes I

Ucluelet

Chemainus

Galiano I

Bamfield

Pender I

Carmanah Valley

Portland I

Port Renfrew

Victoria

0   100 miles

0   100 kilometres

ACKNOWLEDGEMENTS

The authors would like to thank the following people: John Acorn, entomologist and television naturalist; Bill Allen, Alberta Department of Environmental Protection; Ken Bejcar, lodge operator; Scott Benton, B.C. Parks; Shannon Berch, soil scientist; Bruce Bennett, plant adaptation expert; Doug Bowes, Alberta Department of Environmental Protection; Jack Brink, archaeologist; Heather Brook, marine biologist; Shirley Bruised Head, park interpreter at Head-Smashed-In Buffalo Jump; Michael Carroll, managing editor, Raincoast Books; Dick Cannings, ornithologist; Kelly Chapman, bat researcher; Dave Chater, B.C. Parks; Desmond Collins, palaeontologist; Maureen Cumming, B.C. Ferries Corporation; Phil Currie, dinosaur expert; Phil and Marilyn Demers, tornado victims; Johan Dormaar, vision quest researcher; Jonathan Driver, archaeologist; Dennis Dudley, severe weather expert; Tom Ellison, skipper; Tom Fleet, lodge operator; Dick Forbis, archaeologist; John Ford, marine biologist; Bristol Foster, naturalist; Manley Fredlund, helicopter pilot; Don Gayton, ecologist/writer; Paul George, Western Canada Wilderness Committee; Don Gough, B.C. Parks; Brenda Gould, archaeology student; Paul and Audrey Grescoe, writers; Richard Grieve, meteor-impact scientist; Paul and Karen Griffiths, cave experts; Al Harvey, photographer; Janet Hawkwood, geographer/naturalist; Doug Hay, marine scientist; Brian Hayden, archaeologist; Alice Hendry, naturalist/bog expert; Kathy Hickson, vulcanologist; Brian Horejsi, Speak Up for Wildlife Foundation; Chuck Hume, outfitter; Brian Johns, whooping crane researcher; Gary Kaiser, seabird ecologist; Jim Kemshead, Yukon Tourism; Paul Kroeger, mycologist; Pat Kramer, writer; Maureen Landals, sand dunes expert; Paul LeBlond, oceanographer; Peter Lee, ecologist; Brent Liddle, naturalist; Bryan McGill, editor, *Beautiful British Columbia*; Kevin McLaughlin, park warden; Bruce McGillivray, Provincial Museum of Alberta; Bruce MacGregor, forest protection officer; Jeffrey Marliave, research scientist, Vancouver Aquarium; Courtenay Milne, landscape photographer; Peter Mustard, earth scientist; Greg Neilson, cowboy; Cecelia Nesmo, Manyberries farmer; John Nightingale, director, Vancouver Aquarium; Bruce Obee, writer/editor; Richard Padmos, lodge operator; Bill Pagham, geologist; Jill Pangman, biologist/outfitter; Desmond Peters, honorary chief of the Pavilion Band; David Phillips, meteorologist; Betty Pratt-Johnson, diving expert; Heather Pringle, writer; Marilyn Quilley, North by Northwest Tourism; Peter Redhead, lighthouse keeper; Brian Reeves, medicine wheel expert; Joanne Richardson, copy editor; Treva Ricou, librarian; Rod Robinson, Nisga'a storyteller; Garry Rogers, seismologist; Perry Salakin, B.C. Ministry of Environment, Lands, and Parks; Steve Short, writer; Karen Siebold, NWT Air; Daphne Solecki, Federation of B.C. Naturalists; Mark Stanton, president and publisher, Raincoast Books; Shaun Stevenson, North by Northwest Tourism; Duncan Stewart, lodge operator and outdoorsman; Margaret Stoneberg, amateur fossil collector; Charlie Schweger, palynologist; Bob Turner, Geological Survey of Canada; Wanagun, Haida Watchman; Norm Wagner, skipper/outfitter; Dave Wallis, helicopter pilot; Hildegard Westerkamp, acoustic ecologist; Percy Wiebe, Parks Canada; Maywell Wickheim, naturalist/forester; Andy Williams, Helio Courier pilot; Glenn Woodsworth, hot springs expert; Con York, Beaver pilot.

The most beautiful
experience we can
have is the mysterious.
It is the fundamental
emotion which stands
at the cradle of true
art and true science.

— ALBERT EINSTEIN, "THE WORLD AS I SEE IT"

HERE, HIGH ABOVE THE TREE LINE, the land tilts steeply westward. The view encompasses a vast shale-strewn talus slope that runs a half kilometre into subalpine spruce. The forest's highest margins are cut by avalanche chutes and, even now, on this late July day, midsummer snow patches nourish the tiny yellow lilies that grow amid the meltwater. Further down-slope, the valley bottoms out in suitably named Emerald Lake, with the glacier-flanked summit of The Vice President above it to the north. It is not this view but the seemingly unremarkable grey slabs of rock at our feet and the man in blue jeans, with the odd magnifying visor pushed up on his forehead, that have drawn us to this site 2,700 metres up the side of British Columbia's Mount Field. Around us lies the abandoned debris of almost a century of palaeontological excavation, an effort that has unearthed tens of thousands of marine fossils from the mountain's slope to our right. The half-billion-year-old rocks underfoot contain not just *any* fossils but an absolutely extraordinary record of the beginning of multicellular life on the planet. Here on the side of an unspectacular ridge in the Canadian Rockies is the world's most important fossil site and the best record of how life on Earth began. The man standing beside the makeshift plastic-sided hut is garrulous and greying Desmond Collins, 58, the leading expert on the Burgess Shale. He has been showing us his newly found treasures, creatures that are unique – unnamed, unclassified, and stranger than science fiction – things with five eyes, six claws, or seven heads.

As we pass these specimens from hand to hand, it is not hard to imbue them with a sort of spiritual significance; after all, every culture has its talismanic objects and its creation myths. But unlike other artifacts and legends, *these* rocks tell scientists how life *really* began. Holding each of the strange grey-black fossils, listening to an account of their significance, we are in possession of a veritable time machine – one that would do H. G. Wells proud. Time past and time present meet on a stark windswept B.C. mountainside, and the perspective from here encompasses not just the landscape of the immediate talus slope and the surrounding peaks but time itself. This vantage point, this overview, allows for reflection on life's continuities and connectedness.

This, then, is the story of an unusual journey. It is, on one level, an account of a 32,000-kilometre exploration of western Canada. Our meandering route took us past curious signs that read METRIC-FREE CAMPING, JESUS'S DRIVE IN, and WORMS

AND DIRT ICE CREAM. It took us past oddly named Albertan towns, like Chin, Readymade, Skiff, and Manyberries. It was in Manyberries, in fact, that we stopped and chatted with Cecelia Nesmo, a local farmer and widow, who was surprised to learn that her tiny village held the record for being the sunniest place in Canada.

The journey, however, was much, much more than a mosey along backroads, hiking trails, and wilderness rivers. Its itinerary was set by conversations with numerous scientists, naturalists, outdoors people, backcountry outfitters, researchers, pilots, environmentalists, writers, artists, and photographers. Each told us about the natural history, science, or magic of a place that he or she knew very well. Often, as with Desmond Collins, we arranged to meet the expert at the site of his or her obsession. It was like meeting Moses on the mountain. At other times, we followed hand-drawn maps sent to us with details of the particular backroad turns required to find, say, Alberta's remote Sundial Medicine Wheel or British Columbia's unique Farwell Dune. Along the way we also talked with scores of people: a couple who survived the Edmonton tornado described what it was like to look up inside the tornado's funnel; a leading Canadian ornithologist spoke to us one evening about the language of birds; and the first Canadian to climb Mount Everest explained his fascination with verticality.

But we were looking for something more – something elusive, something that is almost impossible to express through scientific data and the mere observation of natural phenomena. Something, in fact, that is almost impossible to express through words. Just as Collins's fossils provide windows onto the nature of time, so each expert, each place, each encounter provided a window – beyond the actual facts – onto things fundamental. And so this is not only a story about nature, it is also a story about a search. By placing ourselves in context – at sunrise atop Alberta's Old Women's Buffalo Jump or amid icy class 3 rapids on the Yukon's Alsek River – we hoped to glimpse, however briefly, something enduring and profound. Each encounter had, we found, the potential to evoke unexpected feelings; each had the potential to provoke insights into those forces that lie at the edge of the unknown.

One doesn't need to be a spelunker to know that Vancouver Island's Q-5 Cave can be an awfully scary place. One doesn't need to be a neo-pagan to appreciate the long-abandoned

Native dream beds on southern Alberta ridges. And one doesn't need to be a humorist to be dumbstruck by the size of fresh grizzly prints outside one's Yukon tent. Just as geology provides an antidote to the millennial hand-wringing popular at this time, so the bizarre Shoe Tree outside Port Hardy, British Columbia, provides a reminder of life's latent absurdities. Just as marsh botany reveals the exquisiteness of the microscopic and the often overlooked, so the fast-disappearing Alberta grasslands speak of attachment and yearning. Archaeology is not just about bones, stones, and grid-lined excavation pits; it is also about humankind's links to the past. Caves are about erosion and deposition, but they are also about myth. Mosquitoes are about blood *and* vulnerability. Cliffs are about glaciation *and* fear. And alpine meadows are about natural succession *and* love.

This is an account of both outer and inner journeys. It is a story about knowing and yielding to the unknown, about close observation and quiet meditation, about pursuit and patience, about conversation and silence. It is, in the end, about that unspeakable place, that triple intersection – not located on any map – where nature, science, and mystery meet.

Time did not exist;
or if it did, it did
not matter.

– MURIEL WYLIE BLANCHET, *THE CURVE OF TIME*

The fundamental things apply . . . as time goes by.

– HERMAN HUPFELD, "AS TIME GOES BY"

Daniel

ABOVE The coast of British Columbia is punctuated with erosional exclamation points. Just as light bends within a prism, incoming ocean waves bend and accelerate around a promontory, striking harder *behind* the point, producing seastacks like these at San Josef Bay. DANIEL WOOD

PAGE 6 Within the old-growth forest of Vancouver Island's Carmanah Walbran Provincial Park stand groves of towering Sitka spruce like these. ADRIAN DORST

SAN JOSEF BAY SEASTACKS NEAR CAPE SCOTT, BRITISH COLUMBIA. Behind us stands the dead spar of a bizarre roadside conifer, its lower trunk covered solidly with hundreds of mouldering pieces of footwear, all nailed to the tree, toes pointing upward. There is no explanation. Behind us, too, is the first 63 kilometres of the thousands of kilometres of backroads we will travel in the months ahead. The muffler took a hit about an hour back, and my Honda became a Harley. That was before I realized I was running on empty, having forgotten to get gas in Port Hardy. I had consoled myself with the thought that there would be gas in Holberg, a town so small that the appearance of its name on the road map is almost metaphysical. That, again, was before we had read the big hand-lettered sign on Holberg's lone set of gas pumps: OUT OF GAS. WE WONT HAVE ANY FOR A COUPLE WEEKS. It was there, contemplating the implications of *that* message, that we met our first mosquitoes. I flattened one and held it out for closer inspection: spread-eagled, it seemed only slightly smaller than my worries about running out of gas.

"Big," Beverley said.

The mosquito-kill seemed auspicious. Thinking of the trajectory of the terrain ahead – Alberta swampland, Yukon muskeg, and B.C. alpine meadow – I said, "The first of –" I searched for a number, a *large* number.

"Of thousands!" Beverley interjected.

"We should keep track. Us versus them, mosquito-kills versus mosquito-bites."

Gasless in Holberg, the competition going in the mosquitoes' favour, we drove on.

Our consolation is that here, at the end of the westernmost driveable road in Canada, in the get-out-the-Gore-Tex rainforest – Cape Scott averages 425 centimetres of precipitation annually – the day is sunny. We descend amid monstrous-leafed skunk cabbage to San Josef Bay. Fallen trees, some with 15-metre-wide roots, testify to the fecundity of the earth and the ferocity of the storms. And the trail map shows 10 shipwrecks offshore. The lighthouse keeper at Cape Scott had said that his wife, Sheila, had stepped out a month earlier into a spring gale and that all 43.5 kilograms of her had gone sideways, downwind, landing unceremoniously in the flower bed. The thought of her flying had amused him.

Our goal on this day, however, is the erosional seastacks at the western end of the bay's enormous white sand beach. There is something about vertical rocks – European megaliths, phallus-inspired Hindu lingams, medieval church spires, even the black obelisk in the film *2001: A Space Odyssey* – that inspires the human imagination. Like the shoes on the roadside tree near Port Hardy, such rocks point up. They contradict gravity.

The principle behind the existence of seastacks is the same as that which operates when a skater at one end of a line accelerates just as the skater at the other end suddenly stops. In other words, ocean waves, too, "crack the whip" – only they do so in a process called refraction. Each incoming wave first hits the shallows of a rocky headland, at which point one section of the wave stops. The rest of the wave, however, accelerates as it wraps around the headland, striking behind the point with even greater force. Erosion, cliffside caves and, in time, seastacks result.

STORM-WATCHING IN A MISERABLE PLACE

Peter Redhead, 46, has had a front-row seat for Pacific storms since he began his career as a lighthouse keeper in 1968. He has, on occasion, felt the earth itself move. Today he and his wife, Sheila, maintain a lonely vigil at Cape Scott, a windswept promontory at the northern tip of Vancouver Island. From this vantage point high above the ocean, they have watched 14-metre-high waves pound the shore, sending sea spray airborne in 35-metre-high explosions. The rocks themselves reverberate. The wind roars. Meteorologists call these incoming storms "Maritime Bombs." Says B.C. oceanographer Paul LeBlond, "This area of the North Pacific has – with the possible exception of Tierra del Fuego – the worst climate on Earth. The highest ocean wave ever – over 30 metres high – was measured by a Canadian buoy off the B.C. coast recently. Every year we get one or two really good storms – hurricane-force winds. Big waves. They're wonderful to look at, but awful to be in." He recommends Cape Beale near Bamfield and Quisitis Point (with its series of surge channels) south of Wickaninnish Beach as relatively accessible places to go storm-watching.

Big waves strike with the force of 42 kilopascals or – in familiar terms – 800 pounds per square foot. Of the hundreds of British Columbia coastal shipwrecks, including five at Cape Scott, virtually none have survived the crushing impact of a few winter storms. MANLEY FREDLUND

At San Josef Bay a half-dozen exquisite seastacks, between five and 15 metres high, protrude from the sand at low tide like black chessmen awaiting repositioning. Wild coastal strawberries, yellow-flowered villous cinquefoil, and red columbine have taken root in the rocks' crevices. Each tower is topped by one or two bonsai-like spruce – wind-warped stunted survivors of coastal storms. Circling the seastacks, I feel like a Lilliputian among the Gullivers. I hope for a message from the rocks but hear only the sound of surf hissing among the shoreline stones. ▦

Beverley

THE SHOE TREE NEAR HAINS LAKE, BRITISH COLUMBIA. Beside the gravel road, our first weird thing: an extraordinary shoe tree. There are rubber boots, cowboy boots, kids' runners (all sizes, all colours), thongs, slippers, one size 20 leather sandal, sneakers, Reebok walking shoes, and hundreds of other pieces of footwear, all neatly arranged, climbing at least halfway up a 15-metre-high tree stump and creeping into the adjacent deadfall like an uncontrollable foot fungus. The brown Hi-Tec hiking boots looped over a nail are, unfortunately, too big. A sign says, JESUS IS WAITING. GIVE HIM YOUR SOUL.

I wasn't expecting the result of our first search for humanity's intersections with nature to be quite so . . . weird. But then, I think, maybe nailing your shoes to this tree is a rite of passage in these parts: a first date arranged, a thesis completed, a divorce

CIRCLING A TRIANGLE ON WINGS

By day Triangle Island, 45 kilometres northwest of Cape Scott, is an unassuming, flat-topped, triangle-shaped hunk of bare rock. No trees. Fog so dense the lighthouse was closed in 1919. By day, another rock in the ocean; by night, a seabird sanctuary. At dusk, forming strange clouds over the sea, thousands upon thousands of seabirds head home, confident that predators – peregrine falcons and eagles – are now winding

down their day's hunting.

Seabirds rule Triangle Island. Thirteen species, perhaps 20 percent of British Columbia's entire seabird population, have managed to work out their differences and nest together, mainly from April to September, on a rock less than one kilometre square. There are half a million Cassin's auklets; 40,000 rhinoceros auklets; 12,000 common murres; thousands of pelagic cormorants, glaucous-winged gulls, and black oystercatchers (with stout

red bills perfect for shucking oysters); huge flocks of white-winged scoters (one of the largest members of the duck family); and tufted puffins, 40,000 of them, all nesting in burrows, forming the largest colony south of Alaska.

Tufted puffins are to seabirds what pandas are to bears. Black, stubby, pigeon-size bodies, white faces with shockingly orange-red parrot-like bills and red-rimmed eyes, long yellow tufts curving down the backs of their heads,

finalized. Maybe it is a simple marking of territory, an "I was here" performed with shoes instead of spray paint, a prank that has snowballed far beyond the imagination of the first person with the first shoe. Footwear nailed to a tree, moustaches drawn on posters, names painted on buses, sealed bottles tossed into oceans, initials carved in bark, petroglyphs scratched in stone – one way or another, people leave their tracks.

I love the tree's oddness. And I wonder: can I get by with one less pair of shoes on this trip? ❖

When humans meet nature, sometimes it is a full-scale, comic collision. Here, outside Port Hardy, a woman's size 8 shoe contains nasturtiums; other shoes contain slugs.
DANIEL WOOD

reminding one of the way a reluctantly balding man combs back his remaining hair. The much less prolific horned puffin – there are only about two dozen on Triangle Island – has eyes that could have been painted on by a makeup artist working on the set of *The Mikado*. Puffins, like pandas, have that indefinable something that renders them more easily anthropomorphized than are others of their kind.

"Triangle Island is far and away the best place to see seabirds in B.C.," says Gary Kaiser, a Canadian Wildlife Service seabird ecologist and part of a team studying the one million birds there. All other ornithologists agree. Much of the scientists' work is done at night when the birds return to reclaim their storm-swept territory. The researchers who live on this rock during the summer months are only too aware of the extraordinary nature of the place and the damage passing oil tankers could inflict upon it.

I want to go deep into the earth . . . I am hungry for the stillness and wisdom of caves.

– STEPHANIE KAZA, *THE ATTENTIVE HEART: CONVERSATIONS WITH TREES*

Beverley

QUATSINO-5 CAVE ABOVE GOLD RIVER, BRITISH COLUMBIA. I am trying to figure out what kink in the labyrinthine twists of Paul Griffiths's hardwiring compels him to squirm around in the bowels of the earth. We are standing on White Ridge, a six-minute helicopter trip from the town of Gold River, at the entrance to Quatsino-5, one of the openings into the deepest cave complex north of Mexico. Griffiths, one of the leading spelunkers in Canada, seems to be kept warm by his passion for caving; in the two-metre-deep snow, he wears a short-sleeved shirt. I wear four layers of clothing and I am cold. This is his environment – a cave system consisting of 10 kilometres of mapped passageways (614 metres underground at the deepest point), and countless more chambers honeycombed inside a marble mountain.

He says his obsession with caving (his B.C. licence plate reads CAVERS) started in the 1950s with the hoboes who lived in a cave near his childhood home in Hamilton, Ontario. But I half suspect that he doesn't have that part of the human brain that triggers archetypal fears of unrelenting darkness, of the disappearance of the sun, of being swallowed up by the earth at death, or of being forced to squeeze through a tight passageway into an unknown world at birth. His psyche, I sense, mirrors that of a high-risk climber's; both are pulled to explore the earth but at opposite ends of the rope.

"Want to go in?" he asks me. Before us is a deep black shaft.

"I don't think so," I reply.

"Where else can you find unexplored territory? What other places are unknown still?" Griffiths asks, as if to tempt me. "Even Mars has been mapped. Even the moon."

He looks across the land from our 1,300-metre perch on White Ridge, at the grid of streets far below, and at the mountains across the valley, all of which have been scarred by clearcutting and transmission lines. "On the surface, it's hard to look out and not see the hand of man on the land," he says. "Underground, it doesn't change. That's why people go caving. They're trying to escape the modern world."

I understand. But I still don't want to go in. ❄

The limestone of north-central Vancouver Island has been eroded by natural carbonic acid to produce over 1,000 caves, including an interconnected series of 600-metre-deep caverns above Gold River. DONOVAN WHISTLER

A tapestry of colour awaits those who explore the hidden underwater world off Nigei Island northwest of Port Hardy. Here a scarlet anemone displays its beauty.
THOMAS KITCHIN/FIRST LIGHT

A DIVE INTO BEAUTY AND TERROR

Betty Pratt-Johnson, 67, has donned mask and tanks to dive the waters of the Red Sea, Great Barrier Reef, Cayman Islands, and Galápagos Islands, but her favourite dive site is Browning Wall at the south end of Nigei Island northwest of Port Hardy. The wall is a 70-metre underwater cliff covered with so much marine life that the rock is invisible, masked by a profusion of colours that are unimaginable from the surface of the dull grey sea. "A tapestry," Pratt-Johnson calls it: pink soft corals, yellow sulphur sponges, mint-green anemones, red urchins, orange-peel nudibranches, and white encrusting sponges. "You never know what you're going to see no matter how many times you go down," she says. Perhaps Pacific white-sided dolphins; Dall's porpoises, one of the ocean's fastest-swimming

mammals; or giant octopi with tentacle spans of up to 10 metres. "The giant ones are friendly and nice," Pratt-Johnson adds. "Not scary."

Not so the six-gilled sharks that usually live at great depths – as much as 250 metres down – but, for reasons unknown, come up from mid-April to late October to hang around the shallow sand-covered shelves of Flora Islet off Hornby Island and Tyler Rock on the west coast of Vancouver Island. "Sometimes my body doesn't tell me I'm terrified until later," Pratt-Johnson says, referring to one Flora Islet encounter. She and her diving partners had flashed their lights about 30 metres down to attract the sharks. Two of them came, ghostly greyish-white creatures, each about 3.5 metres long, and hovered below the divers. Pratt-Johnson was aware that the few things known about these deceptively sluggish sharks

include the following: they react extremely quickly when annoyed, they have exceptionally large teeth, and they are meat-eaters. Intrigued by them and all that is not known about their species, she watched them (and they watched her) for 15 minutes. It wasn't until the sharks swam away and she had almost surfaced that the terror hit her and she vomited it out.

But she keeps coming back, hoping for more close encounters with the 450 different species of fish, the 600 different species of aquatic plants, and the 4,000 different species of invertebrates that inhabit the waters of the B.C. coast. Among her favourite invertebrates are the billowy white cloud sponges. "It's like flying underwater when you go over a cliff and see them – like clouds in the sky," she says. "It's like a reverse world."

You may glance up one day and see by your head-lamp the canary keel over in its cage. You may reach into a cranny for pearls and touch a moray eel. You yank on your rope; it is too late.

– ANNIE DILLARD, *TOTAL ECLIPSE*

QUATSINO-5 CAVE ABOVE GOLD RIVER, BRITISH COLUMBIA. There is, I know now, one thing worse than *going into* a cave and that is *getting out* of a cave. At the snow-covered lip of the 25-metre-deep vertical shaft that opens into Q-5, I begin my version of whistling past the graveyard. I am here because Q-5 is the only known cave in North America with an underground glacier. Having just discovered that my headlamp is controlled by a twisting of the outer cowling, I say to Beverley, "I'll signal if I need rescue. Three short, three long, three short. That's sos, I think."

"Screaming's quicker," she says.

Griffiths attaches my rope, the descender apparatus, and a crotch-clutching climbing harness that wouldn't be out of place in a low-budget horror movie. Then, as I lean over the cave's shaft, he cautions me, "It's where the snow on the glacier turns to ice . . . *that's* the killer."

Beverley says, "Couldn't you have said, 'That's the hard part?'"

I lower myself into Q-5, one of 1,000 caverns in the limestone-rich karst region of central Vancouver Island, the best place in Canada for caving. A hiker, I am; a spelunker, I am not. Blackness, dampness, and sliminess are right up there with coldness, claustrophobia, and vertigo as the six sensations I can, thank you, do without. Descending with the gracelessness of a bag of boiled potatoes, I am facing, I sadly note, all six. At this moment I realize that I like the *idea* of caves but not caves themselves. The idea of prehistoric people hunkered around a fire, occasionally painting mastodons on cave walls; the idea of scribes preserving scrolls in caves above the Dead Sea; the idea of stalagmites and stalactites (whichever is which); the idea of Ali Baba and that concealed fortune: all give caves an aura of mystery. Springs flow from caves. Plato's truths played themselves out in shadow dances on firelit cave walls. Indeed, it seems that, for humankind, Caves 'R' Us.

But the reality of Q-5, when I reach the dimly lit glacier below, is this: I *yearn* for the opaque light in the ceiling far above. Within the cave I can see huge icicles. I can see milky white

calcite formations called moon-milk. I can see where carbonic acid, produced through the interaction of atmospheric carbon dioxide and meltwater, has eroded the soft limestone into a labyrinth of openings that, in descending passages, lead away from Q-5. Standing on the slippery glacier and considering Griffiths's recent warning, I don't want to become any more a part of this cave than I already am. I am not a troglodyte. I haul myself upward toward the light. Gravity, my assistant going down, now becomes my nemesis. The climbing apparatus doesn't seem to work. The rope is wet and icy cold. Ditto the vertical cave wall. Ditto me. When I finally reach the surface, I feel like a man who has just survived a breach birth. ▦

OTHER MAJOR CAVES

▸ NAKIMU CAVES *in Glacier National Park northeast of Revelstoke, British Columbia, have recently reopened to a limited number of visitors after a 60-year closure. The cave system, a major turn-of-the-century tourist attraction near Rogers Pass, is spectacular, having some of the deepest and longest underground passages in Canada.*

▸ CODY CAVE, *located north of Nelson, British Columbia, is an 800-metre-deep cavern, full of stalactites and stalagmites, that is open to the public for regular summertime tours.*

▸ ARCTOMYS CAVE *in British Columbia's Mount Robson Provincial Park is, at 535 metres, one of the deepest caves in Canada.*

▸ CASTLEGUARD CAVE, *located directly beneath the Columbia Icefield south of Jasper, Alberta, is a 20-kilometre-long labyrinth of strange geological features: soda straws, cave pearls, stalactites, a perfectly straight 300-metre-long ice-scoured tunnel, and rivers of frozen ice.*

▸ HORNE LAKE CAVES, *northwest of Parksville, British Columbia, contain some of the best underground formations in Canada. However, the major Horne Lake caves, such as Euclataws Cave with its extraordinary stalactites, columns, and drapes of calcite, are closed due to past vandalism.*

▸ PARKINSON SEAL GROTTO, *a huge cavern located on Vancouver Island south of Port Renfrew, is one of several seaside caves on the Pacific coast that serve as dens for the birthing and raising of the region's seal pups.*

PREVIOUS PAGES In the subterranean world of ice caves, like this one in Haffner Canyon in British Columbia's Kootenay National Park, ice formations may survive year-round, unaffected by temperature changes at the surface.
GRAHAM OSBORNE

No one with an unbiased mind can study any living creature, however humble, without being struck with enthusiasm at its marvellous structure and properties.

Beverley

BRADY'S BEACH TIDE POOLS, BAMFIELD, BRITISH COLUMBIA. Marine biologist Heather Brook, 36, crouches on the black rocks of Brady's Beach beside a small tide pool (best visited during a full or new moon when tides are lowest). A metre long and two-thirds of a metre across, this natural aquarium is covered with bright green sea grass that undulates in the water like a mermaid's hair. The seas that batter this coast – storm waves of five metres are not uncommon in winter – produce higher oxygen levels and more plankton than do calmer waters. This means more sea life. In fact, despite the legendary lushness of tropical rainforests, there are more species of life and more biomass right here – and at places like nearby Botanical Beach and the Queen Charlotte Islands' Burnaby Narrows – than anywhere else on earth. Brook pushes the sea grass aside as though it were a curtain, revealing the world it protects and supplies with oxygen, a world that looks like a miniature garden under glass, each object seemingly placed with care: an ochre sea star, red algae, purple sea urchins, a green anemone, hermit crabs, snails, barnacles, and eight-centimetre-long tide pool sculpins.

Intertidal life is a study in adaptation. Everything here has found a niche in a habitat made challenging by its extremes, a habitat that is, by turns, covered by water, parched by sun, pummelled by waves, and dried by wind. Here, where the environment changes constantly, live some species that have outlasted almost all others. They have done this by mastering a Zen-like existence: they know when to hang on and when to let go.

Take barnacles, for instance. These creatures stick to their guns and anything else they can find. In fact, says Brook, they hang on to the rocks with a glue "dentists would love to understand the molecular structure of." Sea stars grip the rocks, and each other, with suction-cup feet and huddle together, often well above the low-tide line, to preserve moisture. Mussels, with a sticky thread, cling to anything they can, while sea cucumbers make use of tube feet. My way of staying attached to the rocks is to wear Reebok walkers – sans glue, sans suction cups, sans sticky thread, sans tube feet. Brook, better adapted than I am to

this slippery environment, strides confidently to the sandy beach along the seaweed-covered rocks. I feel, appropriately, like a fish out of water.

Something catches Brook's eye, something out of place – an orangeish 20-centimetre-long football-shaped creature that barely fits in her hand. "A chiton," she says. "It'll never survive way up here away from the water." Unlike its neighbours, it obviously does not always cling tightly enough to the rocks. I identify with it. Brook returns the chiton to the ocean and I head for the sand. ❖

My ambition has been to find trees that were bigger and bigger and bigger.

– MAYWELL WICKHEIM

ABOVE "Some people like shopping," says 73-year-old Maywell Wickheim, "but I'm not the least interested in that. I like to see nature just the way it is. I even like bogs." DANIEL WOOD

PREVIOUS PAGES The enormous sunflower star, often more than 60 centimetres wide and ranging in colour from purple to orange, needs to coordinate its 15,000 tube feet to move across the crowded low-tide zone. The British Columbia shoreline, where the sunflower star lives, is one of the world's most luxuriant marine ecosystems. JERRY KOBALENKO/ FIRST LIGHT

THE BIG CEDAR NEAR CHEEWHAT LAKE, OUTSIDE CLO-OOSE, BRITISH COLUMBIA. Sixty-six years ago, when he was seven and growing up in the logging town of Sooke, British Columbia, Maywell Wickheim began his search. In subsequent years he usually worked in the woods: a timber cruiser, a high-rigger, a faller, a log scaler, a bucker, a donkey engineer, a boom man, a chokerman. He did it all. Twelve years ago he heard bunkhouse rumours that local timber cruisers had found some groves of extraordinarily big trees up the coast from Sooke and, since big trees were his obsession, he went bushwhacking. He hasn't stopped since.

We follow him through the dense underbrush, in places thick with salal and sword fern, along a hillside a half kilometre above remote Cheewhat Lake. Bits of fluorescent-pink flagging tape mark the route. It is, as the crow flies, about 65 kilometres to Ucluelet, site of the single rainiest day in Canadian history. Sixty-five kilometres along a different vector is Henderson Lake, site of the rainiest year in Canadian history. This is the rainforest with a capital *R*. Banana slugs the *size* of bananas trace slime trails underfoot. The ground, moist with decay, has the consistency of black tapioca. It is dark, almost abysmal, beneath the forest canopy. Wickheim, bearded and dressed in a red shirt and orange suspenders that read HUSQVARNA CHAIN, plunges through the undergrowth and tightrope walks across moss-covered fallen cedars while I follow clumsily, eyes down like some Christian penitent, like a man approaching the Holy of Holies. Ahead, I know, is Wickheim's prize find: the Alpha and Omega, the Numero Uno, the Big Doodah of trees – something he has been pursuing for 65 years.

"My God!" I say when I finally see the Cheewhat Cedar.

"A tree for tree huggers," Wickheim says. He stands back from the trunk, arms crossed at his chest, an expression of avuncular satisfaction on his face. Here is the man, I tell myself, who wanted to find big trees and did. Here is the man who located the big trees that later became the focus for the environmental battle over British Columbia's Carmanah Valley. And here . . . *here*, unheralded, virtually unknown, seen by only a few people, is the Biggest Tree of All. I look up. I can't see its top. I look at the trunk. It is almost 20 metres in circumference. It is absurdly huge. No one knows its age. Wickheim tells us it could be 2,000, 3,000, maybe 4,000 years old. It could be the oldest living thing on Earth.

I go, Beverley goes and, with arms outstretched, we begin to hug the tree. ⊞

AND THE WINNER IS . . .

Those who seek superlatives among trees have criteria as specific as do The Guinness Book of Records *judges. The tallest tree is not necessarily the biggest; the thickest is not necessarily the oldest. At present the world's tallest tree is the 112.6-metre National Geographic Tree located in California's Redwood National Park. However, the tree described by the American Forests Association as "the world's largest living thing," based on height, circumference, crown spread, and a point system of vital statistics, is General Sherman, an 84.6-metre sequoia, between 2,300 and 2,700 years old, located in Sequoia National Park, California.*

British Columbia's largest trees include:

▸ A 59.6-METRE-TALL WESTERN RED CEDAR, *with a circumference of 19.1 metres, located just above Cheewhat Lake near Clo-oose on Vancouver Island. It is at least 2,000 years old, perhaps 5,700.*

▸ A FOREST OF A FEW HUNDRED TREES *growing on a small island in Vancouver Island's Nimpkish River, at least 50 of which are Douglas firs up to 92 metres tall.*

▸ THE CARMANAH GIANT, *located in Carmanah Walbran Provincial Park. At 96.6 metres, this is the tallest Sitka spruce.*

▸ A 72-METRE-TALL FIR, *with a circumference of almost 6.5 metres, located beside the Chilliwack River east of Vancouver.*

▸ THE RED CREEK FIR, *with a circumference of 12.6 metres, located in the San Juan River Valley near Port Renfrew.*

A HERMAPHRODITE'S SLUG FEST

The rainforest of the Pacific Northwest seems as demented as the imaginings of a madman. It nurtures biological monsters. The branches of coastal conifers are bearded with half-metre-long cascades of cattail moss. The moist ground underfoot is home to more species of fungi – over 10,000 – than anywhere else on Earth. This climate also produces ideal conditions for the only gastropods – the snail and the slug – that have abandoned the sea for the precariousness of terrestrial life. British Columbia has, in fact, one of the world's densest populations of slugs. The King of Slugs (and, indeed, the Queen of Slugs, for the creature is hermaphroditic) is the black-mottled olive-green banana slug, which sometimes reaches 25 centimetres in length. It achieves this size by eating its weight daily, usually in mushrooms, utilizing its 27,000 or so rasping teeth. The banana slug also uses its teeth for a more bizarre purpose: after copulation, which often lasts 12 hours, the entwined slugs chew off each other's penises. This act, called apophallation, is unique in nature.

Woods, that had always meant so much to me, from that moment meant just so much more.

– EMILY CARR, *GROWING PAINS:*
THE AUTOBIOGRAPHY OF EMILY CARR

Beverley

THE BIG CEDAR NEAR CHEEWHAT LAKE, OUTSIDE CLO-OOSE, BRITISH COLUMBIA. Daniel goes one way, I go the other, each encircling the tree with arms spread, measuring with our bodies the circumference of this ancient cedar, leaning into its rough bark, climbing over buttressed roots the size of couches. "Seven," he says matter-of-factly when our fingertips touch on the other side. "Eight," I say, and start to push away from the tree to get an apple from my day pack, to take a picture, to make some notes, to carry on. But I can't. I can not stop. I have to keep going, not to measure but to *touch* this tree, to touch it all, all the way around. My arms open to feel it, my fingers sticky with cobwebs, my foot sinking between massive roots into holes filled with red powder that is now more soil than cedar. Forgotten childhood imaginings of tree-hollow forest creatures nudge my memory like dreams just out of reach. I circle the tree, press my cheek against its scratchy red-grey bark, stretch my arms as wide as I can, wanting the feel of it against my thighs. I mould my body into its curves, stroke its contours like a blind woman exploring the face of her lover. I imagine myself a child again when all trees seemed this big. I press my back into a buttressed hollow of bark and moss and wonder. Why is it that seeing this tree, after scrambling through the bleached bones of the clearcut above, is as sad and wonderful as seeing a tiger? How did it survive the hurricanes, clearcutting, disease, and lightning storms of its lifetime and remain, standing and solid? How does anyone? ✻

There is a crack in everything; that's how the light gets in.

– LEONARD COHEN, "ANTHEM"

Daniel

THE EARTHQUAKE SITE AT PACHENA BAY NEAR BAMFIELD, BRITISH COLUMBIA. At night, beneath a half-moon, the tiny wavelets tumble onto the two-kilometre-long beach at Pachena Bay. For an instant, as each wavelet rises before breaking, the curling wave collects the moon's glow along its entire length, a calligraphy inscribed in silver and then suddenly erased: messages written in light. At my

B.C.'s tallest tree – and one of the tallest in the world – is the 96.6-metre Carmanah Giant, a Sitka spruce located in a remote section of British Columbia's Carmanah Walbran Provincial Park. ADRIAN DORST

WEATHER EXTREMES: FROM FRIGHTFUL TO DELIGHTFUL

- A Wet End: In 1931 a Canadian record of 8,122.4 millimetres of precipitation fell on Henderson Lake, located at the head of Barkley Sound on Vancouver Island's west coast.

- Noah 40, Cape Scott 66: Cape Scott, situated on Vancouver Island's northernmost tip, has the dubious distinction of holding a Canadian moisture record: 66 straight days of precipitation in the winter of 1974.

- The Sky Is Falling: Ucluelet, British Columbia, earned the single-day precipitation record for Canada when 489.2 millimetres of rain fell on October 6, 1967.

- All Wet: Ocean Falls, a B.C. town (population 70) with a doubly wet name, makes it into the record books as Canada's wettest inhabited place. Located on the province's mid-coast, the village averages 4,386 millimetres of precipitation annually. A sign at the town's pier reads HOME OF THE RAIN PEOPLE. Naturally it rains during our visit.

- In October It Gets Worse: Prince Rupert, on the north coast of British Columbia, holds the grim title of being Canada's cloudiest place. It averages just 110 hours of sunshine each summer and 6,123 hours of overcast sky annually.

- Sunstruck: Quaintly named Manyberries, Alberta, is located in the southeastern corner of the province and holds the Canadian record for annual sunshine – 2,785 hours in 1976. The land around Manyberries includes some of Canada's driest, averaging less than 300 millimetres of precipitation annually. The village itself (population 83, up recently from 82 with the arrival of Carl Goddard from Winnipeg) once had many Saskatoon berries and chokecherries but, according to wheat farmer Cecelia Nesmo, they are mostly gone now. It is, appropriately, sunny the day we stop in Manyberries.

- It's a Dry Cold: Canada's all-time lowest temperature occurred on February 3, 1947, when the thermometer at Snag, Yukon, a tiny settlement in the territory's southwest corner, hit minus 63 degrees Celsius.

- It's a Hot Hot: Lytton, British Columbia, and nearby Lillooet share the record for being Canada's worst hell holes. On July 16, 1941, the temperature in both towns hit a devilish 44.4 degrees Celsius.

- Snow Job: The Mount Copeland weather station, located above Revelstoke, British Columbia, recorded 24,460 millimetres of snow during the winter of 1971-72 – a Canadian record.

- Record Fall: At Lakelse Lake south of Terrace, British Columbia, a world record 1,180 millimetres of snow fell in one 24-hour period on January 17, 1974.

- A Hard Wind: During Typhoon Freda, which pummelled the B.C. coast October 12-13, 1962, a gust in Victoria reached a record 144 kilometres per hour. This does not compare to the estimated 400 kilometre-per-hour winds that hit Edmonton during its 1987 tornado.

- Thermometer Rising: At midnight on the night of January 27, 1962, the thermometer at Pincher Creek, Alberta, read minus 19 degrees Celsius. An hour later it read three degrees Celsius. This extraordinary rise of 22 degrees Celsius in just one hour – a record – was caused by a powerful chinook wind blowing out of the Rockies.

- A Soft Wind: The Head-Smashed-In Buffalo Jump area in southwestern Alberta averages 35 days of chinook wind each year, the highest frequency in Canada.

- Hail! Hail! The section of prairie between Calgary and Edmonton is known as "Hailstorm Alley." Twice in the 20th century – in 1901 and 1969 – hailstones 80 millimetres in diameter fell in Edmonton. These official measurements were unofficially surpassed during the Edmonton tornado of 1987 when softball-size hailstones were reported.

back, a driftwood log; beyond that, a line of red alders; beyond that, a Native village of 300 people. The relatives of these Coast Salish people once recorded that a great flood inundated Vancouver Island, covering it to the summit of 1,817-metre-high Mount Arrowsmith. I think of this as I lean against the log. Part of the Native myth, as translated in the Canadian Museum of Civilization's "Notes on West Coast People," describes the fate of the people living at Pachena Bay: "It was at nighttime that the land shook. They simply had no time to get hold of canoes, no time to get awake. They sank at once, were all drowned; not one survived."

For years considered a myth, seismologists now know that the event described above really did occur – at 9:00 p.m. on the night of January 26, 1700. In fact, scientists now know that monstrous subduction earthquakes occur regularly off the coast of British Columbia – once every 300 to 600 years. The tsunami that hit Pachena Bay did not touch Mount Arrowsmith, but the 10-metre-high tidal wave grew in the constant retelling of the story.

As I sit watching the ephemeral messages on the incoming waves, I think of the transient nature of the Earth. Usually things change slowly: by season, by generations, by genetic mutation, by extinction. Every once in a while, however, the message comes *fast*. The people of nearby Port Alberni had no idea what was happening when a four-metre-high earthquake-produced tsunami inundated their shoreline in 1964, destroying 58 buildings. The men in the three fishing boats in Lituya Bay, Alaska, 1,400 kilometres to the north near the B.C. border, had no idea what was happening on July 9, 1958, when 90 million tonnes of earthquake-loosened rock slid from the Fairweather Range into the fjord below. All the fishermen saw was a 550-metre-high tsunami (the same height as Toronto's CN Tower and the highest tidal wave ever recorded) looming toward them. Off the Pacific coast, when the earth suddenly moves, the ocean follows. ▦

BRITISH COLUMBIA'S MAJOR EARTHQUAKES

Seismologists estimate that the 1700 subduction quake off Vancouver Island's west coast registered about Richter 9. Over 20 other Richter 6+ earthquakes, most of them occurring around the Queen Charlotte Islands or off Vancouver Island, have struck in the past 150 years. Here are some notable B.C. quakes:

DATE	PLACE	RICHTER SCALE
1872	Fraser Valley	7.5
1909	Gulf Islands	6
1910	Queen Charlotte Islands	6.8
1918	Vancouver Island	7
1918	Revelstoke	6
1929	Queen Charlotte Islands	7
1946	Courtenay	7.3
1949	Queen Charlotte Islands	8.1
1970	Queen Charlotte Islands	8.4
1996	Vancouver Island	6.3

These are the days of miracle and wonder / And don't cry baby, don't cry.

– PAUL SIMON, "BOY IN THE BUBBLE"

Daniel

HERRING BALL OFF PORTLAND ISLAND IN BRITISH COLUMBIA'S STRAIT OF GEORGIA. A couple of hundred metres off my kayak's starboard side the sky is a tornado of wheeling, mewing, frenzied gulls. Hundreds of birds dive-bomb the glassy ocean in a maelstrom of wings. Propelled by curiosity, I cut to the right, asking myself, what is going on?

The tide in the strait is ebbing and carries me toward the reef off Portland Island's northeast coast and toward the gulls. There is, I realize, *something* in the water. Then I see it: a perfectly spherical silver-coloured ball, over a metre wide, just below the surface. *A floating mine!* I think. Just as the quadruple-espresso blast of adrenaline hits me, I see a metre-long spiny dogfish cut *through* the silvery ball, exiting its far side with a mouthful of fish. I look closely. The ball is a seething, seemingly solid mass of hundreds, maybe thousands, of herring. I watch, agog. I have never seen, or heard of, this phenomenon. It is only after a minute's scrutiny that I see the eyes (and open mouths) of yet more predators. Several harbour seals are gnawing at the herring ball from underneath.

Doug Hay, a herring specialist in Nanaimo, British Colum-

PREVIOUS PAGES These maples and alders in British Columbia's Fraser Valley converge in a tracery of early fall colours. GRAHAM OSBORNE

Here, where the shelving shoreline of Port Renfrew's Botanical Beach meets the ocean, a rare coastal blowhole exhales seawater five metres into the summer sky. TREVOR BONDERUD/FIRST LIGHT

BLOWHOLES: WHERE THE OCEAN GOES VERTICAL

On the rocky west-facing shore of Benson Island, the most exposed island in Barkley Sound's Broken Group Islands off Bamfield, ocean swells funnel into one of the coast's many eroded surge channels, then erupt in spectacular geysers through a small fissure in the rock. It is one of the best blowholes in British Columbia, and it mimics the distant vaporous exhalations of the 20,000 grey whales that migrate past the isolated oceanside bluff each spring and fall. There is a second major blowhole at the northernmost tip of Graham Island in the Queen Charlottes. When viewed in a storm during a brief 15-minute interval on an incoming tide, the Blow Hole, as it is called, below Tow Hill east of Masset goes ballistic, erupting, with a roar, in a 10- to 15-metre-high saltwater explosion. Haida myth says that a whale once beached itself on the rocks there, and all that remains of it is its spouting blowhole.

bia, later explained. Some fish react to a threat by milling. When the school's leader encounters a threat, it turns 180 degrees. The rest follow. The lead fish, not wanting to be vulnerable, turns again. Soon the entire school of fish, often numbering in the thousands, is spiralling in on itself, spinning in an ever-tighter ball as each fish tries to escape the seemingly dangerous margins for the apparent safety of the ball's interior. In most cases, the odds for survival are, in fact, greater in the middle of a herring ball than on its margins, and that is why biologists refer to this reaction to danger as the "selfish herd effect."

Humpback whales have learned to take advantage of the herring school's evasive tactic. Pods of humpbacks ring a school of herring with bubbles, causing the fish to retreat into a ball. Then the humpbacks eat the entire school of fish.

In my encounter I inadvertently play God. I drift over the herring ball, scaring off the predators. The herring resume their more familiar snaking formation, and I sit by myself, dumbstruck, not paddling, alone on the Strait of Georgia – like the Ancient Mariner, contemplating the strange story I now have to tell. ✠

Catherine Hickson saw the sky above Mount St. Helens filling up with roiling clouds, their undersides lit by bizarre blue lightning. "Don't look. Drive! Just drive!" she yelled.

Daniel

THE CARBONIZED TREES AT MOUNT MEAGER WEST OF PEMBERTON, BRITISH COLUMBIA. It is hard for most people, but not for 42-year-old vulcanologist Catherine Hickson, to imagine the catastrophe that once occurred here: an entire mountain exploding; the sky lit by thousands of lightning bolts; the air raining 600-degree Celsius mud and semisolid boulders; the surrounding forest engulfed in ash and enormous avalanches of hot rocks; the Douglas firs half-buried and carbonized, their broken tops flaming like matchsticks.

The land here on this autumn day shows only aspen yellowing along the grey churn of the Lillooet River and the first snow on the serrations of Plinth Peak and 2,604-metre Mount Meager. The sky is calm. But 2,350 years ago, volcanic Mount Meager went ballistic, erupting with the power of 10 hydrogen bombs and burying the valley where we stand under almost 50 metres of pumice and molten rock. The explosion ranks in intensity to

The bald eagles of the Pacific Northwest build the largest nests of any member of the bird family. The largest recorded nest – a "Volkswagen-sized thing," according to B.C. ornithologist Dick Cannings – was three metres wide, 6.5 metres deep, and weighed an estimated one tonne. The reason these nests become so gargantuan is that the same birds may occupy the same location for several decades, adding new half-metre-high walls after the departure of each new brood of eaglets.

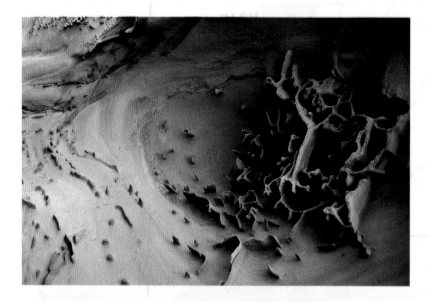

Looking like an aerial view of the walls of an abandoned desert town, this small honeycombed section of Gulf Island sandstone shows the effects of differential erosion. STAN CZOLOWSKI

GALLERIES OF STONE SCULPTURES

The clearest signature of British Columbia's Gulf Islands is the bizarrely eroded orange sandstone bluffs that appear at many sites where the rock meets the Strait of Georgia. In some places honeycombed with thousands of small egg-cup-size indentations, in other places pocketed with womblike shelters large enough to provide comfort to a set of grown quintuplets, these "galleries," as they are called, inevitably cause kayakers to gawk and wonder.

Geologists say the oddly pocked rock is the result of tafone, a process of differential erosion first studied in Corsica. The B.C. formations – considered to be among the best in the world – owe their existence to a series of events. The sedimentary rock itself originates from the late Cretaceous period (90 to 65 million years ago). After the initial compaction of the sand through burial, subsequent uplift, and recent glaciation, a series of sandstone outcrops along Vancouver Island's east coast are now vulnerable to the triple attrition of heat, water, and wind.

The particles of sand are held together with a water-soluble silica and calcite cement that is spread unevenly through the rock. Sea-salt-laden ocean waves, wind-whipped rain, and summer sun assault the coastal cliffs. Water dissolves the rock's softer adhesives, then the sun wicks out the moisture and evaporates the solution. The sandstone becomes sand and an erosional pocket begins in the porous rock. Later, wind scours the ever-growing pocket, enlarging it into a smooth sandblasted cavern. Just as trapped cobbles grind out riverbed potholes, so winds eddying in the sandstone chambers grind and smooth the rock.

Along Hornby Island's Tribune Bay, on Valdes Island's west coast, at Gabriola Island's wave-carved Malaspina Galleries, and around Galiano Island's northernmost Dionisio Point, the solid rock assumes an organic otherworldly curvature, as sensuous as the burnished bark of the arbutus trees that often grow on the clifftops above.

the May 18, 1980, eruption of Washington State's Mount St. Helens. At 8:32 a.m. on that day, Hickson, then a young geology student, watched with her husband as that mountain blew up. Fifty-seven people died; Hickson and her husband barely escaped. The event catalyzed her fascination with one of nature's most awesome phenomena.

As we stand under the now-dormant B.C. volcano beside the Lillooet River, Hickson reads the evidence of the catastrophe in the rock. But what intrigues me – and the reason we are here – are the still-standing carbonized firs that protrude vertically like enigmatic monoliths from the base of the eroding cliff. The searing ash and rock that marked the eruption's initial stage entombed the old trees, which are now revealed as strange 50-centimetre-wide charcoal trunks of Douglas fir, blackened survivors of an ancient firestorm. ▦

THE MAELSTROM OF SKOOKUMCHUCK'S REVERSING TIDAL RAPIDS

Along the fjord-incised coast of mainland British Columbia, the tug of the moon's gravity and the topography of the ocean's bottom produce, in places, a phenomenon that seems to defy physics: the ocean becomes a waterfall. At Seymour, Nakwakto, and Skookumchuck Narrows, the ever-changing tides funnel through the mouths of deep coastal inlets, producing, at full flood, the fastest tidal currents on Earth. At Skookumchuck Narrows, southeast of Powell River, the incoming tide surges through the one-kilometre-wide channel, filling the series of huge inlets behind the opening with almost 500 billion litres of seawater. When the tide turns and the ocean recedes, the water trapped in the inlets can't flow out fast enough. Caught at the narrowing like a liquid being forced through a funnel, the trapped water piles up, rising more than two metres above the adjacent ebbing ocean. Whirlpools form, 100 metres across. There are huge standing waves and whitecaps. Under the moon's invisible tug, the sea becomes a maelstrom. The released water spills between the narrows' bluffs at speeds of up to 30 kilometres per hour, roaring as it sluices seaward.

II THE BONES OF THE EARTH:

BRITISH COLUMBIA'S OKANAGAN, CARIBOO, AND CHILCOTIN

The entanglement of the factors of landscape and love has given us a culture of the West, an urgency, and a closeness to the earth.

– DON GAYTON, *THE WHEATGRASS MECHANISM: SCIENCE AND IMAGINATION IN THE WESTERN CANADIAN LANDSCAPE*

FOSSIL EXPERT MARGARET STONEBERG IN PRINCETON, BRITISH COLUMBIA. There are thousands of them, arranged in the drawers of specially designed cabinets, stored in boxes piled ceiling-high, spilled over the table in this basement room in the Princeton Museum, each containing a cryptic clue to the history of life on Earth. White-haired Margaret Stoneberg, her back stooped almost double with age, pulls open a drawer to reveal a flattened mosquito perfectly etched onto a slab of cream-coloured sandstone by 45 million years of pressure. Then she reveals a birch leaf, a redwood twig, a 20-centimetre-long horse chestnut leaf. Drawer after drawer contains fossils, most the size of the palm of her hand. Some of the rocks are stamped with the impression of plants and trees that no longer live in southern British Columbia: the ginko of China, the katsura of Japan, the sequoia of California. And then Stoneberg retrieves a small fossil, a maple leaf found north of Princeton. The tag in the display drawer gives its scientific name: *Acer stonebergae.*

Although Stoneberg has no formal scientific training, she is, nonetheless, the force that brought the Princeton fossils out of 45 million years of obscurity and into recognition as some of the best plant fossils on Earth. Her hands cradle the fossils, as though by touching them she might be able to unlock their secrets. "They're so beautiful. How can nature make such beautiful things?" asks this tiny woman, who refuses to tell her age. She may be 80, she may be 90, she may be older. But her blue eyes shine with wonder at the things she holds. She tells me the only reason she might want to be young again is to have a lifetime ahead of her to study the Princeton palaeontological sites, to go on more fossil-hunting expeditions.

"My age doesn't matter. *I* don't matter," she says. "There were trees and plants and insects and things 40 or 50 million years ago, and they're still here," she adds, gesturing to the fossil-covered table. "*That* gives me a sense of permanence." ✳

ABOVE "I'm interested in the land," says Margaret Stoneberg. "It gives us food. It gives us life. Everything starts with rocks." DANIEL WOOD

PAGE 34 In the arid alkali lake and grassland region near Kamloops, British Columbia, late autumn burnishes the land with gold leaf. GRAHAM OSBORNE

The stones remember. The earth remembers. If you know how to listen they will tell you many things.

– CLAUDE KUWANIJUAMA, HOPI SPIRITUAL LEADER

Daniel

FOSSIL SITE AT ONE-MILE CREEK NEAR PRINCETON, BRITISH COLUMBIA. I have lugged my old Estwing geology hammer uphill along One-Mile Creek, through fields of fleabane and thistle and along banks dappled with August sunlight. The ground is covered with fallen alder leaves. At a series of low bluffs we have stooped and cracked open the finely bedded white siltstone and shale, revealing the imprints of birch leaves so perfectly preserved – down to the veins and the notches where insects once nibbled – that the decaying modern alder leaves and the fossilized birch leaves mirror each other, bracketing, in one glance, 50 million Augusts.

At the time the Princeton area fossils were first buried, the temperature and terrain were much different than they are now. The region was subtropical, about seven degrees Celsius warmer on average than it is now, with a climate more like that of Los Angeles than that of present-day Princeton. And the land was 1,500 metres higher then. A chain of upland lakes stretched from northern Nevada to Smithers in central British Columbia. Volcanoes dumped millions of tonnes of ash onto the water, interring everything in an oxygen-free silt. Things that normally would have decayed didn't. Instead, they were etched onto the parchment of pale stone with a sepia-coloured photographic clarity: seeds, fish, flowers, flies, mosquitoes, fruit, and leaves. The flowers look as though they have been pressed in the pages of a 19th-century book; the mosquitoes look as though they have just been slapped. In fact, among the 400 species of fossil plants preserved in and around Princeton, many are extraordinary. They record the early history of a number of common species, including the first fossilized evidence of a citrus fruit, the first rhododendron, the first apple, the first cherry, and the first raspberry, as well as the earliest evidence of the arbutus, rose, currant, and mulberry. Here, too, are fossils of the first salmon and the first cedar.

Beverley and I crouch in the dirt beneath a creekside outcrop as the wind riffles the leaves above us. Approximately every fifth slab of siltstone reveals, under the hammer's thunk, a new fossil. We compare our finds. I feel like a kid again, the 11-year-old who bent a few screwdrivers and chipped a couple of his father's chisels looking for palaeontogical treasure. All around

PREVIOUS PAGE Some of the world's premier fossil sites exist in the Canadian West: the plant fossils near Princeton; the fish fossils above Wapiti Lake, British Columbia; the invertebrate marine fossils near Field, British Columbia; and the dinosaur beds of south-central Alberta. GARY FIEGEHEN

us on this warm Similkameen hillside are fossils. In the bluff above us are billions as yet unearthed – little revelations, little connections to the past. I know a few of these fossil leaves will join others already on my kitchen windowsill, daily mementoes, from millions of years ago, of the transience of life. ▣

OTHER MAJOR FOSSIL SITES

▸ HIGH ABOVE REMOTE WAPITI LAKE, *located 60 kilometres south of Tumbler Ridge, British Columbia, the talus slopes contain the fossil evidence of scores of marine creatures, including 20 species of Triassic fish, dating from around 240 million years ago. The preservation of the early sharks, primitive coelacanths, and goldfish is often so complete that palaeontologists can see the impression of scales and living tissue. The site is considered one of the world's best fish fossil locations.*

▸ DRIFTWOOD CREEK, *east of Smithers, British Columbia, contains fossilized* Metasequoia, *an ancient relative of today's redwood. The extensive cliffside site also contains 40- to 70-million-year-old fossil fish, leaves, insects, and ferns.*

▸ AT THE MACABEE FOSSIL BED *just west of Kamloops, and at the Blackburn Mine site high above Coalmont, British Columbia, are fossils similar to those along Princeton's One-Mile Creek.*

▸ IN THE PAST DECADE *Vancouver Island's east coast fossil sites have received a lot of attention. Some of the better-known sites – the Brannen Lake quarry outside Nanaimo, the Chemainus River Canyon near Chemainus, and Collishaw Point on Hornby Island – contain ancient fossilized clams, snails, and spiralling ammonites. The recent discovery of an 80-million-year-old elasmosaur – a ferocious, 10-metre-long marine reptile – in the shale of Courtenay's Puntledge River Gorge was the first of several dinosaur fossil discoveries in the region's riverbanks.*

▸ ON A HIGH SADDLE *below the eroded summit of Castle Peak north of Gold Bridge, British Columbia, lie some of the best fossilized ammonites – the predecessor of today's nautilus – in the West. Some of the spiralling fossils are over 30 centimetres across.*

▸ GRASSY ISLAND *off Kyuquot Sound on Vancouver Island's west coast contains millions of fossilized clams.*

The polka dots of Spotted Lake exist because Epsom salts rise to the water's surface, then later precipitate along the perimeter of roundish pools.
DANIEL WOOD

▸ FIVE-HUNDRED-MILLION-YEAR-OLD STROMATOLITES, *looking like bath sponges, are found in Red Rock Canyon in Waterton Lakes National Park in southwest Alberta. Some palaeontologists question whether the stromatolites were organic creatures; similar primitive patterns, believed to be fossils and found in two-metre-high, 25-centimetre-wide columns, can be seen in the limestone on Mount Dingley in Top of the World Provincial Park near Skookumchuck, British Columbia.*

▸ CASWELL POINT, *on the northernmost tip of the Queen Charlottes' Graham Island, is considered by experts to be one of the most prolific marine fossil sites in the West. Ammonites 60 centimetres across have been found here.*

▸ IN THE LOW PINE-COVERED HILLOCKS *behind the local rifle range northeast of Cranbrook, British Columbia, half-billion-year-old trilobites are regularly found in the red shale.*

▸ PALAEONTOLOGISTS HAVE RECENTLY *unearthed a mass death assemblage of 230-million-year-old dolphinlike ichthyosaurs along the shore of Williston Lake west of Hudson's Hope, British Columbia. It is in the same area as are some of the world's best dinosaur trackways and the world's oldest bird footprints.*

▸ MARBLE MEADOWS, *above Buttle Lake in British Columbia's Strathcona Park, contains limestone outcrops full of various coral fossils that lived when ever-drifting Vancouver Island was once located close to the Equator.*

Daniel

THE GIANT CLEFT ABOVE CATHEDRAL LAKES, NEAR KEREMEOS, BRITISH COLUMBIA. Everything lies below us now – not a sign of civilization, not a person, not a care. Here on the lip of this enormous cliff that rises 300 metres into clear alpine air, swifts ride the thermals, lambent winds that rise up to my vantage point. These birds barrel-roll, silhouetted like black stencils against the sky, and disappear over the ridge top. How high is this cliff? I ask myself. I crawl – I will not risk the gravel underfoot – to the precipice's edge, rocks in hand, and launch my little missiles into space. One thousand and one, one thousand and two, one thousand and three . . . No sound ascends. I peer over the edge, dizzy with vertigo. I watch the next series of pebbles fall and disappear. Millions of years ago volcanic basalt intruded into a gigantic 20-metre-wide subterranean crack in the granite. Uplift and glaciation revealed the rock's flaw. Over the intervening aeons the softer basalt eroded, exposing one of British Columbia's most impressive chasms – the absolutely vertical-sided 200-metre-deep Giant Cleft in the sheer face of 2,621-metre-high Grimface Mountain, located 30 kilometres southwest of Keremeos. Below the spectacular split cliff is Ladyslipper Lake, a surreal-turquoise lake surrounded by alpine larch, the needles of which turn an impossible jasmine-yellow each September. I sit back against a clifftop boulder and drift into reverie. I am one step from suicide as the vicarious thrill of oblivion whispers in the afternoon wind. ⌗

A sacred site could be a cave, rock, a pool, anywhere where a big snake could be or where he comes now and then.

– JACK MCPHEE, AUSTRALIAN ABORIGINAL ELDER

Beverley

THE POCKET DESERT NORTH OF OSOYOOS, BRITISH COLUMBIA. So far Kelly Chapman has overturned 60 rocks. She is determined. She *really* wants us to see a northern scorpion, the only insect in the world known to suckle its young. Or, failing that, a western rattlesnake. What should I expect? I wonder. After all, she has a moon and a bat tattooed on her left shoulder, not because it is fashionable, but because she is a bat expert. "I wanted a western long-eared bat," she says of her tattoo. "It's one of the prettiest ones." The grasses and sage around us are the colour of celadon pottery; the soil is

HOW SPOTTED LAKE GOT ITS SPOTS

One of the most bizarre natural phenomena in the West is 12-hectare Spotted Lake, located in Richter Pass, eight kilometres west of Osoyoos, British Columbia. Unlike most other salty and shallow alkali lakes in North America, Spotted Lake is, as its name suggests, covered in spots. These spots are the result of the repeated deposition of magnesium and sodium salt rings that are formed as the lake's water evaporates each summer. The rings, like low sandbanks, surround circular pools, giving the lake its strange appearance. Natives of the region called the site Medicine Lake and attributed its Epsom and Glauber's salts with the power to heal wounds and to induce youth and wisdom.

sand. We are a couple of hours into exploring the 12,000-hectare Pocket Desert, located on the east side of Osoyoos Lake, just north of Osoyoos. It is the home to dozens of endangered species and, with less than 300 millimetres of rain annually, the driest place in Canada.

Chapman, 29, a specialist in desert life, has a fondness for those strange creatures not high on most people's must-see or must-save lists. There is the desert's five-toed kangaroo rat, which is 65 percent water but never drinks, and the robber fly, which injects its prey with toxic saliva, dissolving the tissues of the unlucky insect so that it can be easily sucked up. There is the pallid bat, which listens for its food – crickets – rather than using sonar, as do other bats. And there is the badger, whose babies' fetal development halts during the winter, when food is scarce, then restarts in time for the kits to be born in the spring. And there is the young burrowing owl which, when threatened, imitates the sound of a rattlesnake. All of these creatures – the scorpion, the rattlesnake, the kangaroo rat, the robber fly, the pallid bat, the badger, the burrowing owl, are threatened and face extinction.

In fact, this tiny area, less than one-twentieth of one percent of British Columbia, contains 22 percent of all the endangered and threatened vertebrates in the province and is one of the three most endangered ecosystems in Canada. More than 250 potentially rare and endangered invertebrate species live here; 23 are not found anywhere else in the world, including three species of sun scorpion that have not even been given scientific names. Seventy-five other invertebrate species that live here, including the praying mantis, have not been found anywhere else in Canada.

"Once this whole area was an old-growth grassland," Chapman says, looking out on what remains of it: a remnant of desert covered with antelope brush, rabbit brush, bluebunch wheatgrass, yellow-flower prickly pear and, near the adjacent cliffs, the Ponderosa. "But it's gone." So are the white-tailed jack rabbit, the short-horned lizard, and countless other species – all earlier victims of encroaching urbanization.

She turns away and we follow her farther into this strange landscape, so different from the postcard images of the Okanagan. "This is my favourite place in the Okanagan Valley," she says. "It feels like it used to feel."

I understand what she means. We survey the sun-blasted earth. And then she bends to look under another rock. ❖

Daniel

THE POCKET DESERT NORTH OF OSOYOOS, BRITISH COLUMBIA. Naturalist Kelly Chapman cautions us to watch where we step: runners aren't the best footwear in rattlesnake country. I think, Yeah, sure. Fat chance, me getting bitten by a rattler. In fact, by day's end, our hike through the desert over, I am complaining about *not* having seen a rattlesnake when a passing man, carrying a plastic Safeway bag at the end of a long forked stick, overhears me.

"Want to see a rattlesnake?" he says.

"Sure."

The man holds the stick toward us. Something in the bag is writhing. He has, he tells us, just caught the rattler by his front door and is returning it to the safety of the desert. We follow, a little brigade of do-gooders, trudging along with a rattlesnake in a Safeway bag. We tell each other snake stories. It feels like a scene from a Eugène Ionesco play. The man releases the snake, and I hear, for the first time, that distinctive brittle rattle – like dry leaves skittering over pavement. Minutes later, on our way back to the car, Beverley says, in a matter-of-fact voice that comes from just behind me, "Another one."

Another what? It is a thought that is interrupted by a frighteningly fast movement at ground level to my right. I whirl. A second rattlesnake, about 1.5 metres long and the same distance away, has slipped out of the roadside culvert and is quickly slithering directly toward *me*. Jesus Christ! I think. The words are not framed as a prayer. I make an adrenaline-fuelled vault of Olympic proportions, and the man with the stick prods the snake toward the safety of the culvert on the far side of the road. ⊞

YE WHO GAZE UPON THIS ROCK / THINK YE WELL BEFORE YE WALK / UPON THE HILLS AND SHALE SO STEEP / FOR IF YE FALL YOUR KIN SHALL WEEP! Inscribed decades ago, this admonition on a Pocket Desert boulder fails to warn against rattlesnakes.
DANIEL WOOD

It takes a shock – a sudden burst of beauty – to wake us to the wonder of our reality.

– CANDACE SAVAGE, *AURORA*

Beverley

BIRD-WATCHING WITH DICK CANNINGS AT VASEUX LAKE, BRITISH COLUMBIA. I realize, just after Daniel and I have doused ourselves with as much mosquito repellent as we can handle without gagging, that Dick Cannings, 43, is a man obsessed. We are walking a path at the marshy northern end of Vaseux Lake near Oliver, British Columbia. Every so often Cannings stops and, for no apparent reason, cocks his head slightly, takes a notepad from his hip pocket, and scribbles: catbird, oriole, chat, cedar waxwing. I have yet to see a single bird. Affable red-haired Cannings, one of Canada's leading bird experts, admits to this peculiar habit: almost every day he writes down the name of every bird he sees or hears. He averages 20, sometimes 40 different birds daily. And he has done this for 16 years.

Fifty metres ahead on the muddy path, Cannings's nine-year-old son Russell, a huge butterfly net over his shoulder and a pair of oversize binoculars around his neck, waves at me. He pulls the branches of the red-osier dogwood aside and there is a tiny bird – a yellow warbler, he whispers to me – flitting back

Almost half the planet's four million or so western sandpipers use the Pacific coastal flyway on their annual migrations. Some flocks of these shorebirds number 100,000.
ADRIAN DORST

and forth less than a metre away among the neon-green leaves. Its fist-size nest, packed with down and straw, contains three tiny cream-coloured eggs. We continue on the path, Russell calling out the names of the birds he notices. And I struggle to shift my way of seeing, hoping to perceive a flash of wing before it comes into view or an unusual density in the leaves.

As we walk over to the cliffs across Highway 97 from Vaseux Lake, the only place in Canada where canyon wrens are found, I ask Cannings how many different bird calls he knows.

"About 500 North American birds," he says.

"Five hundred!"

"I have trouble with the eastern warblers. I always get their accent wrong," he says apologetically.

Daniel says, "I know *one* bird call." And he attempts a pigeon's coo that sounds more like a man blowing bubbles through a straw.

Cannings then makes the real sound.

I say to Daniel, "You speak pidgin pigeon."

Cannings offers to speak canyon wren to "get one singing." He soon receives a reply from a white speck on a boulder 100 metres away. He says, somewhat dismissively, that all he is communicating to the bird is: "I'm a canyon wren." But as the two of them call back and forth, a duet of man and bird in the quiet final moments of the day, it is as though they are opening a door between two worlds. And the language of birds is their key. ❦

BIRD-WATCHING SITES

▸ VASEUX LAKE, *a shallow four-kilometre-long wildlife sanctuary in British Columbia's southern Okanagan, is known for its diversity of species. The eroded cliffs above the lake are home to thousands of white-throated swifts and canyon wrens. The dry terrain nearby has more species of raptors than does anywhere else in Canada. And the lake itself is home to tens of thousands of waterbirds.*

▸ BEAVERHILL LAKE, *65 kilometres east of Edmonton, is probably the best bird-watching site in Alberta. Over 250 different avian species have been recorded here, and some of the migratory birds, both waterfowl and shorebirds, arrive each spring and fall in flocks of 10,000 to 20,000. At times pelicans inhabit the lake's northern end.*

▸ JUST NORTH OF SQUAMISH, *British Columbia, up to 3,000 bald eagles – one-fifth of the province's entire population – line riverside trees during the annual late autumn salmon-spawning migration.*

▸ BOUNDARY BAY, *south of Vancouver, is one of North America's premier birding habitats. Literally millions of birds may be found here: an estimated 500,000 sandpipers gather in the early fall; tens of thousands of loons, grebes, gulls, and ducks feed each March during the annual herring run; thousands of enormous and raucous migrating snow geese arrive in flocks of 25,000 each October; and 130,000 or so ducks winter here thanks to the region's mild climate.*

▸ BECAUSE OF THEIR HEIGHT AND RELATIVE COOLNESS, *the Cypress Hills of eastern Alberta are visited by 200 different species of birds, including the rare wild turkey.*

▸ DURING APRIL, 20,000 *brant, migrating from Mexico to the Arctic, stop in the shallow waters off Parksville, British Columbia. They join dozens of other migratory species, including 2,000 rare trumpeter swans, to refuel in this central section of the Strait of Georgia.*

▸ SOUTHEAST OF CAMPBELL RIVER, *remote Mitlenatch Island has the largest seabird population in the Strait of Georgia. Of British Columbia's estimated 16 million seabirds, many utilize this protected spot for nesting and rearing their young.*

▸ ALMOST 220 AVIAN SPECIES *have been recorded at Inglewood Bird Sanctuary on the Bow River, just east of Calgary.*

The range of what we think and do is limited by what we fail to notice.

— R. D. LAING

NIGHTHAWKS AND OWLS IN THE PONDEROSA ABOVE VASEUX LAKE, BRITISH COLUMBIA. Evening is a good time for predators and a bad time for prey. It is a good time to see owls. The ponderosa pines, their bark deeply corrugated and smelling distinctly of vanilla, are scattered across the grassy Okanagan hillside, allowing the twilight to filter down among the trees. Our guide, Dick Cannings, tells us his father took him bird-watching as a child and that he knew how to use binoculars long before he knew how to bicycle. He calls himself "a twitcher," birder's lingo for a person who enjoys checking birds off his Life List. So far he has sighted 2,300 North American species plus uncounted hundreds of Latin American birds.

As we walk, he says that the trick to seeing things – birds, in his case – is to have a "search image": a half-recognized blob in a tree or on a rock, a particular movement at the periphery of sight. I realize I have heard this from other scientists – people who observe, not through the casual scan of the novice, but through the experienced appraisal of the expert. As we walk, the sky metamorphoses from salmon to pink, to mauve, to purple. I observe scenery; Cannings observes birds. A shape has a meaning to him, a sound a name. I am secretly annoyed at myself because I have two eyes and two ears, but I am obviously not tuned to the correct frequency. I want to know birds, too.

As we walk, at regular intervals the air suddenly fills with a hollow otherworldly *whooompff* – a sound reminiscent of that made by a morose musician drawing his bow across the bass string of a fiddle.

"Nighthawk," Cannings says. We are standing, the three of us, in the darkening forest, and Cannings holds his arms out, then flairs his fingertips and arches backward, mimicking the nighthawks' courtship plunge. "Whooompff," he says in imitation.

"Whoof," I say. But I can tell from Beverley's expression that I am better at dog than at nighthawk.

We climb into thicker forest where Cannings has mounted some of the 250 nesting boxes he has placed in this region. It is almost dark. The nighthawks have ceased booming. Ahead Cannings stops and gestures, and I see that he is pointing at a small curious blob – a blob with two eyes, perched atop one of his nesting boxes just 10 metres away. He tells us it is a baby saw-whet owl. Cannings imitates its sound. I keep my mouth shut this time. The owl says nothing. It stares. We stare. In our binoculars, enormous eyes. The minutes pass. Nothing moves. Stillness and silence. Contact across the species. ⊞

What do I believe in? I believe in sun. In rock. In the dogma of the sun and the doctrine of the rock.

– EDWARD ABBEY, DESERT ANARCHIST

Beverley

THE FALKLAND HOODOO AT PILLAR LAKE, BRITISH COLUMBIA. I look at Daniel. His jaw is slack. He looks at me. Then we both look at *it*. "I'll be damned," I mutter, which is only slightly more articulate than Daniel's "Wow!"

Now I know why I had an odd sense of pilgrimage as we climbed up the steep 15-minute trail from the backroad north of Falkland, British Columbia. Nature's rarities – bizarre, solitary, little-known, and logic-defying – do that to me.

Before us is an erosional pillar, a single 30-metre-high hoodoo that thrusts far above the forest in a column of mortared cobbles and sand, topped with a precariously balanced boulder the size and shape of a Volkswagen bus. It looks completely out of place, stark and phallic among the dark green pines.

"Differential erosion," Daniel says. "There used to be a ridge here, but it's all been eroded away . . . except for *this*. The boulder protects the column underneath from the wind and rain." But we can't figure out why the elements haven't eroded the five-metre-wide pillar away from the sides where, in some places, the clay is powdery.

To us, the existence of this hoodoo is puzzling. But it wasn't puzzling to those local Natives who once saw the world through myth and told the story of To-no-ana, who loved to paddle her canoe on the lake below. Over time, the spell of the water spirit, Ton-ug-nik-nik, compelled her to join him in his underwater world. Her parents were grief-stricken when they found their daughter's empty canoe. Ton-ug-nik-nik, concerned that he had caused such sadness, crept up to the lakeshore and built a gigantic pillar with a huge boulder at the top. He summoned To-no-ana's parents and told them to weep no more because their daughter was happy. He vowed that if he ever caused her the slightest fear, the balanced rock would fall and he would return her to them. ❖

HOODOOS

▸ ONE OF CANADA'S MOST BIZARRE *geological formations lines the cliffs of British Columbia's Wokkpash Gorge, located in a remote valley north of Fort Nelson near the Yukon border. Thousands of hoodoos, some with huge boulders balanced atop*

An eight-tonne boulder – defying, it seems, gravity and logic – balances atop this improbable nine-story-high sentinel near Falkland, British Columbia. DANIEL WOOD

When dinosaurs roamed the lowlands near Drumheller, Alberta, 75 million years ago, the vast and shallow Bearpaw Sea covered much of central North America. Remnants of ancient coastal beaches are, in places, now eroded into surreal five- to 10-metre-high hoodoos.
DANIEL WOOD

skinny 100-metre-high eroded columns, fill the canyon along five kilometres of river.

‣ THE STUBBY, BANDED HOODOOS *outside Drumheller, Alberta, owe their existence to extremely hard sandstone concretions that cap the pillars, protecting the softer sandstone beneath from millennia of wind and water.*

‣ A SET OF FIVE IMPRESSIVE *clay-conglomerate hoodoos above the Deadman River north of Walhachin, British Columbia, are capped with harder overhanging rocks that balance atop 15-metre-high columns.*

‣ THE LEANCHIL HOODOOS *along Hoodoo Creek in British Columbia's Yoho National Park display preposterously balanced boulders atop towers of sand, silt, and clay.*

‣ A HALF-KILOMETRE-LONG ERODED CLIFF *north of Canal Flats, British Columbia, contains a number of 70-metre-high conglomerate hoodoos that line the site where Dutch Creek enters Columbia Lake.*

‣ MANY KILOMETRES OF TOWERING SANDSTONE HOODOOS *and natural bridges, some bearing ancient Native petroglyphs at their base, flank the Milk River in Writing-on-Stone Provincial Park in southern Alberta.*

THIRTY-METRE JELLYFISH AND OTHER SUPERLATIVES

‣ The smallest bird in the West is the seven-centimetre-long calliope hummingbird.

‣ The West Coast's lion's mane jellyfish sometimes reaches an incredible size: a metre across its body and tentacles 30 metres long.

‣ The western white pine bears only a few cones per year, but these reach a record size for this region: 30 centimetres.

‣ The pygmy shrew is this region's – and North America's – smallest mammal. The endangered animal weighs in at four grams and has a length of eight centimetres.

‣ British Columbia's bracken ferns have been measured at up to five metres in height.

‣ The speed at which a diving peregrine falcon has been clocked by a team of B.C. zoologists, using a radar gun, is a mere 128 kilometres per hour. This is less than half of a long-held estimate of the fastest bird's top speed.

‣ The longest-lived animals in the region are the river-dwelling white sturgeon (over 150 years), the geoduck clam (120 years), and the rockfish (120 years).

‣ Alberta's pronghorn antelope is the world's fastest land animal. Over sustained distances it is even faster than the cheetah. It can cruise at 55 kilometres per hour and can accelerate, in short bursts, to over 110 kilometres per hour.

‣ The chiton, one the world's most primitive molluscs, reaches a record size on the B.C. coast: some brick-red gumboot chiton grow to be a half-metre in length.

‣ The arctic tern has one of the world's longest annual migrations – from its summer home

I remember when the world made more sense.

– VAN MORRISON, "TAKE ME BACK"

Daniel

KEATLEY CREEK ARCHAELOGICAL SITE, NEAR PAVILION, BRITISH COLUMBIA. I am trying to imagine what it was like here 1,200 years ago. This empty field was a village then, and kekulis (roofed pithouses) dotted the slope above the river now called the Fraser, below the mountain now called Tom Cole, near the Interior Salish village now called Pavilion. All that remains, it seems on this cool summer morning, is a hillside full of strange circular hollows, 115 in all, that mark the site where 1,500 people once lived. Their descendants include, quite possibly, the man in the Confederate Army hat – with its insignia of crossed rifles – who is walking ahead of us, eyes to the ground. It is not, I know, shyness that bends 64-year-old Desmond ("Dez") Peters's head. It is artifacts, evidence of his ancestors' presence amid the pine and sagebrush above Six Mile Rapids. Father of 11, grandfather of too many to count, former chief of the Pavilion Band, and possessor of a brand-new Simon Fraser University certificate in Native Studies, Peters is, without trying, giving me a lesson in observation.

"Many people walk over things," he says, bending down.

Dez Peters's mother-in-law, Celestine Edwards, once lived in a five-metre-deep Interior Salish pithouse not unlike those that sprawled for 1,350 years above Keatley Creek, British Columbia, until a calamity struck in 850 A.D. DANIEL WOOD

in Canada's high western arctic, along the B.C. coast, to its winter home on the coast of Antarctica.

▸ The appropriately named salmon-orange sunflower starfish of the B.C. coast is the world's largest: some have been measured at a metre across. With as many as 44 rays and up to 40,000 tube feet, it can move at an unstarfishlike speed of three metres per minute.

▸ The leaf of a particularly huge Pacific Northwest skunk cabbage was measured at 130 centimetres long and 72.5 centimetres wide. This is far larger than the record 90-centimetre leaf of a bigleaf maple and the 45-centimetre leaf of the bog-loving devil's club.

▸ The sea kelp and bull kelp of coastal British Columbia, annual seaweeds, grow from being microscopic to being 40 metres long – all in a single summer. The sea kelp, growing 30 centimetres per day at its peak, is the fastest-growing plant on Earth.

▸ The largest antlers of a mature male elk have been measured at 1.5 metres long and 1.8 metres wide.

▸ The white sturgeon of southern British Columbia, once plentiful and now endangered, reaches a gargantuan size. One, caught in the Fraser River in the 1890s, was 5.5 metres long and weighed 630 kilograms.

The spiral – inward into a whirlpool's vortex, outward into a galaxy or, as here, upward into a pine cone – is a visible manifestation of the fundamental centrifugal and centripetal forces. AL HARVEY

The old pictographs and abandoned village sites below enigmatic Farwell Sand Dune are all that remain of the local Shuswap people, wiped out by smallpox in 1862. Now there are only ghosts. DANIEL WOOD

When he stands, he shows us a half-dozen sharp black chips of rock that he has extracted from the bunchgrass. "From Cache Creek," he says, locating the original source of the flakes 50 kilometres to the east. "From Arrowstone Mountain. Black basalt. People were knapping flint here." I look down. Where I see pebbles, Peters sees speckled chert, obsidian, and black basalt, material that was once part of an intricate trading system that made Keatley Creek one of the largest known prehistoric villages in the Pacific Northwest.

Archaeologists, digging at the site over the last 10 years, have discovered that Keatley Creek arose in 500 B.C. as a centre of trade and wealth, a position it assumed because of the abundance of salmon in the river below. They also know that the village, one of over 1,000 prehistoric sites in the British Columbia's Upper Hat Creek region, was suddenly and inexplicably abandoned in 850 A.D. In time, the stick-and-sod pithouse roofs collapsed, burying the dwellings' multiple hearths, the tools, jewellery, baskets, bone, and debris of 1,350 years of occupation. The Natives themselves forgot about the place. But drawn to this strange field full of pits, archaeologists have teased the site's history from the land.

I walk away from my companions, trying to merge my knowledge of the scientific with the land itself. Spikelets of meadow barley attach themselves to my socks, and daisylike mountain sneezeweed encircles the 20- to 30-metre-wide pits that, 2,000 or so years ago, were homes. Each pit is surrounded by a low earthen mound where thousands of fragments of worked stone still lie. Grasses and reeds grow in the bottom of many of the pits where rainwater collects. As I descend into one of the shallow craters, dozens of tiny white butterflies erupt before me like transitory harbingers of the dead. I recall that the Greek word for *butterfly* and for *soul* are identical: *psyche*.

The women who once dug this hole were probably slaves. They used the shoulder blades of deer as shovels and served the village's aristocracy well. For over 1,000 years, archaeologists know, little changed. The salmon came each summer, as did the traders. Flint was knapped, baskets woven, and shells drilled into buttons. The sun shone. Of the labour it took to dig these enormous pits, of the labour it took to transport the trade goods, of the dozens of generations that once lived here, Peters had said earlier: "Time meant nothing then." I sit with my back to the pit's circular wall and, looking up, see that the sun is now encircled by a hazy iridescent ring. The past and the present encompass me beneath a circle of desert sky. ▩

Night is the Time of the Goddess . . .

– MARTHA GRAHAM, *THE NOTEBOOKS OF MARTHA GRAHAM*

Beverley

FARWELL SAND DUNE OUTSIDE RISKE CREEK, BRITISH COLUMBIA. Eight California bighorn sheep stand in silhouette against the darkening sky, poised on the ridge line, reminding me of the china animals that paraded along my childhood shelves. I take the sheep's picture, they stare back at me, then turn and run away. I smile but can't shake the fear that began as soon as the road dropped out of the Chilcotin grassland and into the eroded badlands along the river. I feel that I need to find a place to hide, but I don't know from what. There is nowhere to escape this feeling of dread, of not wanting to have my back to the strange dune, or to the road that switch-backs up the other side of the canyon, or to the river that snakes around our tent, or to the huge hoodoos that stand against the cliff wall and serve as ghostly reminders of all those who died here during the 19th-century smallpox epidemic – an entire tribe wiped out. We cook our supper, battle mosquitoes, arrange sleeping bags, but normalcy doesn't comfort me; an inexplicable sense of foreboding insinuates itself into the lonely place. We paint our names with sparklers against the night sky, and I try to laugh but want only to hide. I have never been afraid like this before – without reason, without antidote.

I lie awake, my flight-or-fight response in high gear. But there is nothing to fight, nothing to flee – except this feeling of danger, a spell cast by the alchemical combination of this bizarre

SAND DUNES: SURVIVORS FROM THE ICE AGE

Unlike British Columbia, with its solitary and magnificent Farwell Sand Dune, Alberta has a number of unexpected desert features. The desolate Middle Sand Hills between Medicine Hat and Empress, the dry zone south of Grande Prairie, the huge expanse of sand in Wood Buffalo National Park, and the low dune fields around Opal are all remnants of large, post-Ice Age sand dunes that have crept, pushed by prevailing northwest winds, over the province during the past 10,000 years. Until recently these dunes were gradually disappearing in the face of agriculture and increasing vegetation. Global warming may change this, as temperatures rise in the West and as the Prairies dry out. The most impressive dunes in Alberta are the remote Athabasca Dunes south of Fort Chipewyan near the Saskatchewan border. There, a single parabolic dune, seven kilometres wide and 13 kilometres long, is moving southeastward at a rate of one metre per year, inundating a boreal forest of jack pine and black spruce. Wags have calculated that, based on its speed and trajectory, the slowly moving dune will soon leave Alberta and, in another three million years, bury Ottawa.

landscape, my imagination, and who knows what other forces of nature. A terror grips my psyche and insists on having its way. I am compelled to keep watch, to sit up and stare through the mesh opening of the tent into the blackness with no idea of what I am looking for or why. I turn on my flashlight and feel as if I am taking a huge risk of being seen by whatever it is, whoever it is. But I *have* to look at my watch to know how many more hours until daylight and, I hope, freedom. It is 3:30 a.m.

I do not sleep. ❖

Daniel

FARWELL SAND DUNE OUTSIDE RISKE CREEK, BRITISH COLUMBIA. Everything tells me the thing before us is completely wrong: a big sand dune in the middle of British Columbia. Seen from below, at the bottom of Farwell Canyon, the dune appears small, a curving arc atop the hoodoo-punctuated cliffs along the boiling grey-green Chilcotin River. Seen up close, the enormous dune swells like a Saharan mirage. But it is real . . . even surreal. And that makes its proximity all the more compelling. The prevailing westerlies, caught in the vortex of an impressive oxbow in the river's gorge, have scoured the canyon's soft clays and limestone and driven the eroded silt and sand upward, over the clifftop, creating a scimitar-shaped 300-metre-long dune that rises 50 metres above the surrounding grasslands.

I set my foot tentatively on the lee edge of the dune. Beverley follows reluctantly. Her face has a haunted expression, as though the unexplained ghosts of the previous night are still near. I feel like a trespasser here: the dune is unscarred, pristine, arching up like a huge bone-coloured brontosaurus's back, filling half the sky. Every step seems an insult, a Vibram-soled kick against the sand's untrammelled perfection. I reach the dune's spine and tightrope-walk higher along its hard-packed edge. To my left the rippled surface drops steeply to sage, bunchgrass, and sand-engulfed pines; to my right it drops equally steeply to the hoodoos and swirling river far below. When we reach the highest point, we stop, balanced on the knife edge like two existential acrobats suspended in time. We do not speak. The possibility of slipping is real, and the vantage point too strange for words. I know, as we turn to descend, that the wind will quickly erase the transitory evidence of our footsteps. Nature always has the last say. ⊞

The Chilcotin River's white water hisses far below. The sand also hisses, propelled by the wind. The huge dune moves leeward, away from the canyon, burying the ponderosa pines in its path. CHRIS HARRIS/ FIRST LIGHT

BRITISH COLUMBIA'S KOOTENAYS, THE ROCKY MOUNTAINS,
AND ALBERTA'S FOOTHILLS

The river flows
on like a breath,
in between our life
and death. Tell me:
who's the next to
cross the borderline?

RY COODER, "ACROSS THE BORDERLINE"

*That which we do not bring to consciousness
appears in our lives as fate.*

Daniel

**AMONG THE BLUE DARNERS IN CRESTON MARSH,
WYNNDEL, BRITISH COLUMBIA.** When I was very young,
dragonflies held, for me, a particular horror. They could,
someone had told me, *sew up your mouth*. For years, as a 20th-
century victim of this medieval superstition, I fled the speedy
insect – as I did most insects, in fact – believing in their inherent
capacity to do evil. (Ladybugs were the exception.) Yet here I
am, walking the mosquito-infested dike north of Wynndel's
Duck Lake, trying to look at them with the eye of a scientist
while wishing I could kill most of the pesky little buggers
around me.

John Acorn, 39, an Edmonton biologist and TV broadcaster,
had earlier tried, with limited success, to convey to me the source
of his lifelong delight in bugs. As an entomologist, his specialty
is, among other things, dragonflies. He perceives beauty, I realize
as I listen, where I sense furtive movement and incipient danger.
Of the 80 or so dragonfly species in Canada's West, he says,
"They're these weirdly shaped things. They're superbly coloured.
They're big and graceful and fast. You look at them and you
know they're looking at you." Yeah, I think, hearing this, they're
looking at my mouth!

We have walked along the dike for 17 nanoseconds when
the first electric-turquoise dragonflies appear – 10-centimetre-
long blue darners. Their aerobatic movements, like those of
hummingbirds, seem to defy the fundamental principles of
physics.

"Run! Hide! Cover your lips!" Beverley says.

"Hope they sew up *your* mouth," I tell her.

I know from conversations with Acorn that these insects
are descendants of prehistoric monsters: dragonflies with 70-
centimetre-long wings. (Now *that* would be scary.) I know, too,
that today's creatures – the fastest insects on Earth – are capable
of attaining speeds of almost 100 kilometres per hour. I am
pretty sure, though, that they won't be sewing up anybody's
mouth. So I try to see the dragonflies as Acorn sees them. In this
7,000-hectare marsh live several thousand different insect
species, a galaxy of miniature creatures that I barely know and
usually try to avoid. I recall that, at the same time I was terror-
ized by childhood encounters with dragonflies, I treasured, as

PAGE 58 The profusion of colours,
shapes, and varieties of alpine wildflowers reaches its zenith on British
Columbia's mountain slopes in the
first weeks of August. A visitor to
this high world grows almost giddy
from the kaleidoscopic vistas.
GRAHAM OSBORNE

most kids do, small things: stamps, tadpoles, toy trucks, tin sol-
diers, pond-water whirligigs seen through my Junior Scientist
microscope set, and rice grains – displayed at Ripley's Believe It
or Not in Old Orchard Beach, Maine – that were decorated with
entire Chinese landscapes. Having listened to Acorn and having
considered my lifelong dragonfly phobia, it occurs to me that the
world is full of small, overlooked mysteries. The panoramic so
often obscures the microscopic. What size, after all, *are* the angels
that dance on the head of a pin? Are they an electric blue? Can
they fly backward? Do they mate in the air like dragonflies? 🈳

Dragonflies are a cross
between a helicopter and
Cruise missile. They hover, fly
backward, and can accelerate
to tremendous speeds. With
20,000, six-sided lenses in each
eye and 360-degree vision,
they are lethal – to their prey.
IAN LANE

LANDSLIDES: WHEN TERRA FIRMA ISN'T

Across the mountainous regions of the West, the steep slopes bear evidence of what happens when gravity overwhelms terrestrial inertia. And geologists, reading the details of the cataclysm in the landslide debris, can assess exactly what occurred. In the winter of 1855-56, near Whistler, British Columbia, an estimated 25 million cubic metres of volcanic rock broke loose from The Barrier, a 500-metre-high cliff that formed when the molten lava of a Pleistocene volcano collided with an Ice Age glacier. The 19th-century landslide, racing downslope at almost 100 kilometres per hour, cleared away trees 80 metres above the valley bottom of suitably named Rubble Creek. Elsewhere, outside Spences Bridge, British Columbia, the lower sec-

tion of a mountain slid across the Thompson River in 1905, damming the flow for four hours and killing five people. In 1965, following a minor earthquake beneath 1,983-metre-high Johnson's Peak located east of Hope, British Columbia, the entire side of the mountain – a one-kilometre-wide slab containing 46 million cubic metres of snow, rocks, and forest – slid into the valley, burying four people. Ten years later 2.5 million cubic metres of meltwater-loosened ice and volcanic rock swept down from Devastation Glacier west of Pemberton, British Columbia, killing four geologists. All four sites are clearly visible today.

By far the most impressive landslide site in the West is the enormous fan of rocky debris left from the famous 1903 collapse of Turtle Mountain in

southwest Alberta. At 4:10 a.m. on April 29 of that year an estimated 30 million cubic metres of limestone, loosened by the inherent weakness of the rock and by coal mining under the mountain, fell on the town of Frank. In 90 seconds three square kilometres of valley bottom lay beneath a layer of rocky rubble that was, in places, 30 metres deep. Seventy people died. The site, even now, is a vast, barren, virtually impenetrable maze of huge and jagged grey boulders, tombstones for the town of Frank and memento mori of a night the earth moved.

In the past century 385 people in the West, including 70 here at the former site of Frank, Alberta, have died beneath massive landslides and avalanches. The Frank Slide is a graphic reminder of gravity's power over topography. DANIEL WOOD

If you have an obsession, you have a wonderful life.

– HANNA PINDER, WILDFLOWER EXPERT

AMID ALPINE WILDFLOWERS IN THE BUGABOO MOUNTAINS WEST OF SPILLIMACHEEN, BRITISH COLUMBIA. The helicopter departs and we are soon alone on the crest of a barren ridge enclosed by a phalanx of icy 3,000-metre summits and an indigo sky as transcendent as the inner dome of a Greek church. We have nothing more strenuous to do today than stroll downhill five kilometres to the hundreds of thousands, or maybe millions, of blooming wildflowers that fill Septet Basin below. Up here, high above the tree line, the mineral-laden soil is thin and grey. The colours run to pewter: the gravel, the schists, the blotches of lichen. This is how Canada looked at the end of the last Ice Age. But to quote T. S. Eliot: "Time the destroyer is time the preserver." And proof of this axiom lies beneath our feet. Low tufts of moss campion, its pink all the more vibrant amid the otherwise lifeless alpine tundra, are the first hint that natural succession – and summer – has begun to colour in this stark frontier.

In the high mountains of the West summer is a brief interregnum: the last snow of the passing winter falls usually in early July and the first snow of the coming winter arrives in late September. In the two and a half months between snow and snow, literally trillions of alpine flowers explode sunward across the West in one of the planet's greatest displays of seasonal colour. The first colour wave in late July begins amid the stunted spruce at the tree line and the grassy south-facing ridges released from winter's cold blanket. Small yellow avalanche lilies, often growing on mossy meltwater-saturated slopes, climb upward as the

Multihued varieties of paintbrush transform the alpine slopes of the West into Impressionist canvases that stretch in places to the horizon and contain, literally, millions of wildflowers. T. GELDSETZER

snow retreats. Elsewhere come tiny pale spring beauties and cream-coloured western anemone, known to some poetically as "windflower" and to others by a more fanciful metaphor: "hippie-on-a-stick." By the time this initial pale-coloured bloom wave has crested the ridges, the second, and far more vibrant, wave of late-blooming alpine flowers has erupted. The scarlets of Indian paintbrush, the purples of lupine, the yellows of buttercup, the nacreous pinks of clover, the orange-reds of columbine, the lavenders of fleabane, the whites and creams of daisies – the eye is assaulted as entire meadows and hillsides are transformed into seemingly airborne Persian carpets. A single glance encompasses 25 different floral species, hundreds of colour variations, and 10,000 flowers.

By lunchtime we have found a couple of brookside rocks to lean against and succumb to the visual onslaught of countless flowers. I have a thoroughly perverse, and probably uniquely male, urge to go berserk and run, shouting like Alice's nemesis, the Queen of Hearts: "Off with their heads!" as I decapitate the flowers because they are so . . . so *insistent*. Instead I lie back, as Beverley does, with the sun on my face and join the flowers, turning like a heliotrope toward the one true god of the True North – the sun.

Charles Darwin's theory of survival of the fittest is fundamentally challenged at the Burgess Shale site. The fossils here seem to show evolution occurs through survival of the luckiest. Each day during summer digs here about 60 extraordinary invertebrates, dating from life's beginnings, are found. Visitors to the quarry have said, "This is where God touched the Earth." DANIEL WOOD

Mindful of such paleontological wonders as large dinosaurs and African ape-men, I state that the invertebrates of the Burgess Shale . . . are the world's most important fossils.

– STEPHEN JAY GOULD, *WONDERFUL LIFE: THE BURGESS SHALE AND THE NATURE OF HISTORY*

Daniel

BURGESS SHALE FOSSIL QUARRY ABOVE FIELD, BRITISH COLUMBIA. We are climbing *up* to the bottom of an ancient ocean, like some latter-day wayfarers going to see Moses and his mountain. The Moses in this arduous four-hour trek is Desmond Collins, a world-famous Canadian palaeontologist, and the mountain is Mount Field, high in British Columbia's Yoho National Park. Decades after I had abandoned childhood dreams of unearthing tyrannosaurs, and decades after my university geology professor had spoken in awe of the fossils on the mountain above Field, British Columbia, I finally reach the site where Collins and his team of assistants are helping to rewrite the first chapter in the history of life on Earth. The air reverberates with the clang of sledgehammers striking steel chisels and, in turn, chisels striking rock. The ground is littered with discarded flat shards of shale. Around us in the six-metre-deep quarry are the world's most important fossils.

The marine creatures that are preserved on this high ridge provide a glimpse ("a window," Collins calls it) of what life was like on the ocean bottom during the Cambrian period, 515 million years ago. It was a time before anything lived on the land. The fossils here were preserved so perfectly that even soft-bodied creatures like primitive jellyfish are revealed in near-photographic detail. More important, the variety and the complexity of these first animals show that, from its very beginning, life on Earth exploded with possibilities. Nature, a half billion years ago, was experimenting with form; surrealism often reigned. There are things here with five eyes, or six claws, or seven heads. *Hallucigenia* for example, had a bulbous head, seven pairs of pincer-tipped legs, seven more pairs of spines, and six small tentacles by its curved and hollow tail. All the phyla of animals known today, including the first chordates (from which humans are descended), are here. More amazingly, there are 15 species of animals that fit into no known classification, no phyla – creatures so phantasmagorical that they seem to have arrived directly from the Star Wars Café.

Collins takes us to his makeshift plastic-sided hut and retrieves from canvas specimen bags his summer's prizes, including

THE BLOOD OF THE EARTH

It is easy enough to imagine that where the ground appears to bleed, people have imbued it with sacredness. For centuries the Natives of the Kootenay Mountains came to three cold springs that still bubble from a hillside fault in the iron-rich rock 80 kilometres northeast of Radium Hot Springs, British Columbia. The mineralized water issues iron oxides and iron sulphides that colour the springs' vents and adjacent marshland in otherworldly sulphur yellows, blood reds, rusty browns, and milky greens. Natives of the Rockies once mined the mounds of brick-red precipitates that surround the pools. They formed the clay sediments into small pancakes that were first baked and then traded across the West. The Plains Indians used the powdered cakes for war paint, teepee decoration, and clothing dyes. The tribes of the B.C. interior used them for painting pictographs. Today a walk amid the 250,000-square-metre site between suitably named Ochre Creek and the Vermilion River provides a glimpse of a time when people knew nothing of the Earth's chemistry, calling the bizarre paint pots Usna'waki-cabugi (Place Where the Red Clay Spirit Is Taken).

a dozen animals that have no name and no history because they have never been seen before. There is aptly nicknamed Squid-on-a-Stick, Spiny-Thing Three, and a five-centimetre-long sea moth that Collins compares to a tiny jet fighter. I hold the unique fossils, secretly fearing that I will drop the damn things and send palaeontology back to the Stone Age. "You find something completely different," says Collins. "It's better than Monty Python. The really best moments are when you've found a couple of bits and then you find something that puts it all together. Suddenly all the pieces fall into place. You know – wow! That means this and this means that . . . and it all falls together."

This, I tell myself, is what propels the scientific search; the moments when the pieces fall together. Eureka. Satori. Synthesis. Enlightenment. Oneness. Epiphany. Nirvana. The words try to contain the ineffable quality of revelation, the instant when the parts become the whole. I hold Spiny-Thing Three for a while, hoping its odd shape has a secret to reveal to me. It *is* beautiful. It *is* enigmatic. But all I get is dirt on my hands. ▦

THE METAPHYSICS OF MOUNTAINS

Mountains have broken me and healed me.

– LAURIE SKRESLET, MOUNTAINEER

The summit of Mount Laurie, also known by its Native name, Mount Yamnuska, rises above a wide 350-metre-high cliff beside the highway east of Banff, Alberta. It is the first rockface 46-year-old Calgarian Laurie Skreslet ever climbed, and it is one he has climbed a thousand times since. He has bivouacked on its sheer limestone face and listened to the night's silence. He has been there when lightning bolts exploded on its 2,500-metre peak. He has seen people fall there, and he has seen people die there. Yet he keeps returning (it does, after all, bear his name), testing himself against the mountain he loves above all others. To him, it is a friend.

Skreslet climbs mountains because he likes to put himself in situations that are easy to enter but hard to exit. In such circumstances, he says, he must force himself to reach, to go beyond his self-imposed limitations. On a mountain his fate is in his hands. Beyond the personal challenge that mountains offer him, Skreslet believes that they reward him in a deeper, more spiritual, way. The chiaroscuro of light and shadows, the weirdness of strata contorted by tectonic pressures, the sheer verticality of upthrust earth, the perspective from summits: these link him, in some profound way, to time out of time, worlds out of world. Mountains have made a mystic of him.

On top of a mountain, says Skreslet, the first Canadian to climb Mount Everest, "My gaze takes in thousands of square kilometres and that huge expanse opens me up. The land, the vastness becomes part of me. I become part of the land. Mountains are broken places, part of the Earth that's broken. They're places where people go to break old patterns, to change the things that make them stiff. You go there and skim the shit away and begin to see your soul."

The raw wilderness that is just over the mountain rim . . . is the edge of my dreaming.

— JACK SHADBOLT, ARTIST

Daniel

THE WILDLIFE OF YA HA TINDA, SOUTHWEST OF SUNDRE, ALBERTA. Except for the moose cow eyeing us from the margin of the lodgepole pine, there is nothing to indicate what lurks in the surrounding wilderness. We have only the testimony of 35-year-old Greg Neilson, the cowboy who herds, breaks, and trains the 150 head of domestic horses here at 4,320-hectare Ya Ha Tinda, a federally owned ranch linked to the National Parks Service. Around us on this summer's day the rolling grassland of this immense intermontane prairie runs to the wedge-shaped, over-thrust mountains of the eastern Rockies. Blue-green shadows of cumulus ride the fields eastward into the aspen and pine. Dozens of teepee rings lie hidden along the banks of the nearby Bighorn River. Hidden, too, are the mule deer, the wolves, the grizzlies, the coyotes, the bighorn sheep, the wild horses, and the extraordinary herds of elk – the largest concentration of such herds in Canada.

Neilson has driven us in his four-wheel-drive pickup – with a half-dozen blocks of blue tongue-sculpted salt licks in back – out across the grassland and parked in a vast field. He is a man who dislikes cities and city ways. (He tells us that once, at the Calgary Stampede, someone congratulated him on the authentic look of his "cowboy outfit.") Standing there in his frayed canvas jacket, blue jeans, big belt buckle, pointy-toed boots, and Stetson hat (which, when removed, reveals an untanned forehead), he is, in fact, the picture of cowboyness. He tells us he loves the land here, loves the place's isolation, loves riding horseback, but he admits that his wife, SueEllen, is less enamoured than is he of the rural ranch life 90 kilometres from Sundre.

He says they hear wolves all the time. Coyotes, too. And mule deer and grizzlies regularly pass the ranch house. The 200 wild horses, however, are leery of humans and keep to the distant meadows. But elk? Oh, yes, he sees elk. He points to an unnamed hill in the near distance. The previous fall, he says, while riding with another cowhand through the leafless aspen along the hill's base, they found themselves amid some scattered elk. "All of a sudden, we looked up an' that whole hillside started to move. I dunno. There had to be at least 3,000 elk. We tried to count 'em, but you couldn't. That whole hill looked like an anthill. It was neat. We just sat there . . . *amazed*."

FOLLOWING PAGES "Sometimes on a winter night when the moon's out," says cowboy Greg Neilson of the Ya Ha Tinda Ranch, "the elk come. Hundreds, maybe a thousand of 'em. We turn out the house lights. They come through the trees – black shadows moving against the blue snow. It's pretty unreal."
DANIEL WOOD

I study the hillside, now green and motionless. I confess: I feel envy. C'mon God, I think, send out the elk. Nothing. One lethargic moose. And then Neilson adds, as though to gall me further, that in winter the elk sometimes surround his ranch house, and he and his wife turn out all the lights and watch the black silhouettes moving silently over the blue snow. "Sometimes there's moonlight," he says of those moments, "and you can see almost forever."

I liked the way he qualified "forever." He didn't want his perspective to sound too self-satisfied. ⌘

THE CALVING GLACIER AT MOUNT ROBSON'S BERG LAKE, WEST OF JASPER, ALBERTA. We have, I assure myself, *worked* to get here. Twenty-two kilometres of serious backpacking, a nine-hour climb, a 790-metre elevation gain punctuated with the occasional encouragement of descending hikers: "It's worth *every* step."

Yeah, I had thought grimly, easy to say. You're going down and we're going *up*.

That is all past now, forgotten. There is a picnic lunch to be eaten and a view that is considered by many to be the most spectacular in Canada. As I look out, a few wispy banners of cirrus fly above 3,954-metre Mount Robson, the highest peak in the Rockies. From its snow-covered summit, the mountain's face falls two kilometres in a near-vertical wall of rock. From the mountain's flanks, two crevice-riven tongues of blue-white ice – Mist Glacier and Berg Glacier – form pincers, holding aquamarine iceberg-dotted Berg Lake in their grasp. A small iceberg-glette has grounded so close on the lakeside rocks that Daniel breaks off a crystal chunk, which we gnaw on.

It is this vantage point that we have worked so hard to attain, not only because of the spectacular surroundings, but also because here the effect of global warming is obvious. The two glaciers are clearly, even audibly, *melting*. In fact, recent tree-ring measurements have shown that, throughout the Rockies, the icefields have shrunk in the past 150 years by an astonishing 25 percent. (During the same period, the planet has warmed by one degree Celsius.) Across the lake the treeless, gravelly moraine that marks the farthest advance of Mist Glacier now forms a gigantic empty *U*. The glacier itself has retreated over a kilometre in recent times. But it is Berg Glacier that is the real attraction. Its crevices, we know, regularly issue thunderous

Nearby Berg Glacier and more distant Mist Glacier tumble from the flank of Mount Robson. This view is the reward for a day's strenuous hiking amid huge waterfalls and icy summits too numerous to count. The view is also a window on global warming.
ART WOLFE

sounds, as the ice fractures and slides beneath the summer sun. And, we have been told, on occasion its 800-metre-wide and 20-metre-high toe releases a slab of ice directly into the lake. We have come here to witness Berg Glacier calve. We want to see the Big Splash.

Lethargic from lunch, the alpine sun, and the previous day's hike, we lie back, eyes slitted, when we hear an enormous whoosh! Did it calve? Did we miss it? No. Offshore one of the nearby drifting icebergs has noisily heeled over. We watch it bob. Then fate rewards our efforts. As we watch the iceberg, a section of Berg Glacier peels off and hits the lake with a tremendous splash. It looks like a white explosion.

"Didja see it?"

"Yeah. Did you?"

"Did you?"

I lean back against a lakeside boulder, half-drunk with the panorama and the sun, with a sense of well-being so complete that it is almost dangerous. Okay, God, I think, Take me now. ❀

Yellow pond lilies hang suspended like a galaxy above the obsidian water of British Columbia's Ellerslie Lake. GRAHAM OSBORNE

IV   SHADOWS AND CIRCLES IN THE GRASS:

SOUTHEASTERN ALBERTA

Everywhere I
look I see fire;
that which isn't
flint is tinder, and
the whole world
sparks and flames.

— ANNIE DILLARD, *PILGRIM AT TINKER CREEK*

The world tells you to look for truth in grotesque combinations.

– SAUL BELLOW, NOVELIST

Daniel

THE PETROGLYPHS AT WRITING-ON-STONE, EAST OF MILK RIVER, ALBERTA. Archaeologists say that this is the place the dead were brought to. Local Piegan Natives, members of the Blackfoot Nation, believe it is the place where their ancestors' ghosts still reside. The bodies were trussed to the branches of the big cottonwoods lining the Milk River below and were lodged in the caves in the eroded sandstone cliffs above. Nearer to the sky, the dead could see the distant Sweetgrass Hills, blue-black silhouettes on the horizon, and, upon going there, reach paradise. The story is old, its roots lost in time. No one knows the dates for this place. No one knows its purpose. Even the Blackfoot call it Aysin'eep (It Has Been Written) because it existed before they came. Sometime during the past 3,000 years nomadic plains buffalo hunters arrived in this bizarre hoodoo-filled valley and recognized, in the otherworldly landforms, a site suitable for ceremonial transformations and storytelling. Using sharpened bones and antlers, they began writing on the stone. Today the site contains the largest collection of Native rock art in North America.

As I follow crop-haired 37-year-old naturalist Janet Hawkwood along a section of the seven kilometres of petroglyph-covered sandstone cliff, she stops again and again to offer her interpretation of the thousands of stickmen images, geometric shapes, dream creatures, and modern graffiti – one example of which reads ELVIS PRESLEY – inscribed on the rock. Here are centuries-old depictions of warriors with thrusting flag-draped spears. Here are chimerical spirits with symbolic "power lines" radiating from their heads. When the first horses appeared in the region in the 1720s, they were recorded in the petroglyphs as bearing shield-carrying attackers who battle running Blackfoot warriors. Here is an intruder – a 19th-century white man judging by the Abraham Lincoln-style top hat – and here a covered wagon, and here, ominously, a whiskey bottle. All these phantasmagoric of images, from ancient spirits to contemporary lovers, flow together.

I study the half-metre-long petroglyph of a buffalo and a mythical dream beast nearby. From the dozen deep pockmarks in the sandstone animals, it is clear some modern-day marksman has targeted them. Like the first RCMP officers who added

ABOVE Now only kestrels and rock doves occupy the cliffside caves at Writing-on-Stone Provincial Park where once the predecessors of the Blackfoot left their dead and etched thousands of stylized images, like this 19th-century stagecoach, into the canyon walls. DANIEL WOOD

PAGE 74 No archaeologist has been able to translate the meaning, or even figure out who made, many of the thousands of exquisite petroglyphs at Alberta's Writing-on-Stone Provincial Park. The site contains the continent's largest collection of prehistoric art. DAWN GOSS/FIRST LIGHT

their names to the prehistoric images, like the hundreds of inscriptions of modern visitors who have, illegally, recorded their presence, the marksman found a way to leave his peculiar message on the stone. The wildly eroded cliffs take on, in the early evening, the appearance of skulls. The hoodoos assume the looming shapes of ancestral ghosts. Cottonwoods follow the valley's meandering, and through it a milk-coloured river runs as spectral as bone.

There is no scientific explanation for the petroglyphs. This makes the place all the more eerie. Toward the end of our walk, acknowledging the conflict among archaeologists regarding the site's history, Hawkwood says, "People come here and they provide different narratives about the land. It's the way we internalize the unknowable. We give it *our* story, *our* interpretation. Then, we walk *into* our narratives." I write this down, another enigma to consider. ⊞

OF VISION QUESTS, DREAM BEDS, AND STONE CIRCLES IN THE SKY

Across southern British Columbia and Alberta, the Kootenay and Blackfoot peoples once sought, through vision quests, a personal connectedness to natural forces. Much like the better-known walkabouts of Australian Aborigines, the Natives of this region believed that the young, primarily boys between the ages of seven and 19, needed to find a spiritual identity. This rite of passage into adulthood was facilitated, they felt, through isolation, thirst, hunger, and yearning. After a sweat lodge ceremony and instruction from the tribe's elders, the youth would set out alone and either find or build a dream bed atop a mountain summit or a prairie hill.

Lethbridge's Johan Dormaar, a 67-year-old amateur archaeologist, has located about 75 of these sites in southern Alberta. In his dream bed, a small hollowed-out oval pit lined with a low stone wall to provide protection from the wind, the young person would lie down and wait. Prompted by four days of fasting, he would entertain visions. Sometimes a totemic animal would appear, sometimes a dreamlike hallucination. Often the dream beds overlooked a prominent landform, which would focus the mind and produce a sense of attachment. The looming blue-black Sweetgrass Hills on the Alberta-Montana border, 2,787-metre-high Crowsnest Mountain in the southern Rockies, and sheer-sided Chief Mountain in Waterton Lakes National Park

are three such landforms still encircled by ridge-top dream beds. At the end of the quest the youth would descend, describe to the elders his vision, receive guidance about his future role within the tribe, and often take a new name. Today these ancient dream beds are usually overlooked by those who travel with backpacks and bug repellent. But they are there, inviting the discerning to lie down, to daydream, and to seek a connection to the Earth.

Says Dormaar of his findings: "The sites are always elevated so you can see more. Both sunrises and sunsets. A lot of sky. Maybe that's the point of a vision quest – to see more, to look with a long view."

My sense is that we've reached the age where science and the arts can be consenting adults, that they can cohabit with one another without jeopardy to either one. The interface between science and the arts is, to me, the wave of the future.

– DON GAYTON, AUTHOR, RANGE ECOLOGIST

Beverley

GRASSLANDS OF THE CYPRESS HILLS, SOUTHEAST OF MEDICINE HAT, ALBERTA. This 2,600-square-kilometre plateau straddling the Alberta-Saskatchewan border is a reminder of how things once were on the Canadian Prairies and of how much is gone. The hills are a topographic anomaly: 1,466 metres at their highest point, these uplands have the distinction of being the highest place in Canada between the Rocky Mountains and Labrador. The Cypress Hills first appeared to us as a mirage on the horizon, then as a bulging blue-grey silhouette, then as a doorway into an ecosystem dramatically different from the one we had just driven through. They contain forests – lodgepole pine, white spruce, balsam poplar, aspen – a dozen species of grass, and summertime temperatures 10 degrees Celsius lower than those on the scorching prairie below. Range ecologist Don Gayton, 51, author of *The Wheatgrass Mechanism*, had, a few days earlier, described the Cypress Hills as "a geographical clasp, a buckle that holds North America together." It is the only prairie landform not scraped by glaciers, where the creeks on the south side flow into the Gulf of Mexico and the creeks on the north side flow into the Arctic Ocean. A confluence of forces.

Here at Horseshoe Canyon, where Daniel and I walk under midsummer's evening sun, Gayton had studied the patterns of the grasslands for hours. Down on hands and knees, he had observed each blade: this one is spear grass, this June grass; this one wide, this narrow; this one greenish, this blue. He had then stood up to distinguish them from a distance of three metres, then 10 metres, then 30 metres. Now he can glance at an entire hillside and spot exactly where northern wheatgrass blends into western wheatgrass, a change from a three-millimetre-wide leaf to a four-millimetre-wide leaf and from green to blue-green. "There's something enduring and humble about grasses that I find very attractive," he had said of his obsession. "Here's an organism that can withstand phenomenal fluctuations in temperature and moisture and survive over the long term." The vagaries of nature, I had thought, are one thing, but the neglect

TEEPEE RINGO: STONES WITH A STORY

Along the coulees and escarpments of southern Alberta, hundreds of Plains Indian teepee rings survive as overlooked circles of stones amid the prairie grasses. (The stones held down the hides covering the teepees.) Thousands more have been destroyed by modern agriculture. The smaller three-metre circles probably date to the time prior to 1725 when the Blood and Piegan peoples used dogs to transport the teepee poles and hides. The larger seven-metre circles probably date to later times when the horse, capable of hauling longer poles and larger loads, had appeared on the Prairies.

engendered by a limited aesthetic sense that values only the obviously spectacular is quite another.

It was near here, Gayton told us, that he had found a Native dream bed, a depression in the ridge top where a young person once had lain during a vision quest, and where Gayton himself had also lain, plagued by the what-if-someone-sees-me doubts inspired by Western culture's separation of the scientific and the spiritual. "The Chinese have the philosophy of *feng shui*, that forces of the Earth coalesce in certain areas," Gayton had said. "Well, they damn sure coalesce in the Cypress Hills."

I sit, as did Gayton, on the canyon's clifftop, an almost vertical precipice where a landslide once dropped a section of the hills onto the plains below. I stare out across the prairie, imagining it untouched by human hands and covered with grasses rippling in the early-evening wind. This is the land with which I formed what Gayton calls my "primal landscape bond." It is the land in which I grew up, and which has become, even after decades of living elsewhere, a subconscious reference point, the place that my psyche recognizes as Home.

I am suddenly overcome with grief. For the buffalo, the plowed-under wheatgrasses and depleted soil, for a long-lost prairie childhood, for I don't know what. I lie in a little hollow at the edge of the cliff and weep into the grass, thinking only: Have I turned my back on this land just as so many others have? ❖

Chief Sitting Bull fled the United States after defeating General Custer in 1876, retreating northward to the region of Alberta's Cypress Hills where buffalo still survived. Today the prairie's grassland, except in protected parkland, is empty of buffalo. DANIEL WOOD

DEEP ROOTS IN AN UNFORGIVING LAND

The humble grasses of the Canadian Prairies, like the people who live there, provide lessons in endurance. The grasses live amid temperatures that fluctuate annually from minus 40 degrees Celsius to plus 40 degrees Celsius. They flourish in constant wind and in occasional summer-long drought. There are short grasses that thrive in dust storms and only 30 to 60 centimetres of rain per year; there are others that grow to be two metres tall and have a root system just as deep. One crested wheatgrass plant was found to have a network of roots that would have measured 600 kilometres if each root had been laid end to end. Where it is too moist to be desert and too dry to be forest there is grassland. But the adaptability of grass and the richness of its soil has, in some ways, brought about its downfall. The 10- to 20-centimetre-deep chocolate-cake soil of the Canadian Prairies is among the most productive soils in the world, so it was the first to be turned. Furthermore, prairie grass had adapted to the plains bison, its life cycle accommodating that animal's migratory grazing in midsummer, fall, and early winter. Consequently this grass is devastated by the spring grazing and year-round trampling of beef cattle. Almost all of Canada's grassland has now been taken over by agriculture or ranching. In fact, there are only a few hundred hectares of original tall-grass prairie left, virtually all of it in southern Manitoba.

On the prairie, one twists around and around until the straight horizon line turns into its opposite, a circle, and the visual turns visionary.

– GEORGE MELNYK

Beverley

THE SUNDIAL MEDICINE WHEEL OUTSIDE CARMANGAY, ALBERTA. No one we talk to, not even the one-toothed woman behind the bar, has heard of the medicine wheel. We had thought it would be simple. Drive to the medicine wheel, have a look at it, drive northwest to camp at Old Women's Buffalo Jump, have supper. But no. What started out as a curious side trip has become a quest for a little-known site – a quest that began with a faxed, half-decipherable map we had received from some archaeologist somewhere. We cross the empty prairie, scanning the horizon, stopping, checking the map. There is no one to ask. It is hot. Dry. Windy. And mosquitoey. Thousands of them spiral together in five-metre-high tornadoes, buzzing outside the window when we pause to get our bearings. *X* marks the spot on the map of the Sundial Medicine Wheel, but where is *X* out there?

Finally, after turning onto ever-narrower dirt roads and driving a kilometre across rutted grass, we step out of the car into barren windswept prairie. Nothing for miles around. It feels the way church is supposed to feel but usually doesn't. We climb the steep hill, together but alone, to Sundial Medicine Wheel, described to us as the best surviving medicine wheel in Canada. At the top two concentric circles of lichen-covered stones

PREVIOUS PAGES From this vantage point the southwest-facing entrance passageway of the Sundial Medicine Wheel crosses two low concentric rings of stones toward the rubble of the central cairn. DANIEL WOOD

ANCIENT MEDICINE WHEELS: THE CENTRE OF THE CIRCLE

Across the northern Prairies, from South Dakota to southern Alberta, more than 80 medicine wheels lie abandoned and half-forgotten, visited only on occasion by archaeologists and a few Natives but always by the ever-present wind. Of the hundreds of these circular patterns of hilltop stones that once dotted the Alberta plains, only 50

survive. (Another dozen survive in Saskatchewan.) Archaeologists who have investigated these strange rings – some of which form large concentric circles, some with as many as 28 radiating spokes, some with two-metre-high central cairns – are not certain about their significance. Native elders can't explain them, either. These rings have no apparent celestial purpose, no alignment to any particular compass direction.

From stratigraphic evidence, from the finding of human bone beneath some cairns, and from the size of slow-growing lichens on the exposed rocks, most of the medicine wheels are believed to be hundreds, maybe thousands of years old – the work of the buffalo-hunting Blood Indians. The last one was constructed in 1940.

The finding of skeletal human remains at a few such locations indicates that some of

surround a low, rocky cairn. Someone put these rocks here maybe 2,000 years ago, but no one knows why. We know that, on occasion, Natives come to pray here, to make offerings, to conduct personal rituals. I feel a bit like an intruder. I am not sure what to do.

I walk around the perimeter of the 27-metre-wide outer circle. The wind, the sky, the history, the unanswered questions evoked by the site fill me with a growing sense of this place's sanctity. Why is this ancient pattern of stones here? I walk around again, this time following the 17-metre inner circle of stones that encloses the central cairn. Was this made to honour a great chief? I circle again. Who were the people who placed these boulders? What did they think about? What did they feel?

I stand at the entrance to the central cairn, in an aisle delineated by boulders, and feel like an ill-prepared bride. I had wanted to bring an offering here but had no tobacco, no sweetgrass. All I have is a bunch of wilting cilantro extracted from our Styrofoam cooler. I start up the aisle, feeling strangely self-conscious, as though the ghosts of buffalo hunters are watching me. I circle the cairn, placing sprigs of cilantro on the lichen-covered rocks, saving the biggest bunch for the very top. I feel sobered, hushed. The only thought that surfaces is, Thank you. Thank you to those who constructed this strange wheel, to those who use it, to those who protect it, to those who, like me, find ways, however clumsy, to touch the earth here and feel strangely moved by the hilltop's mystery. I look out across the prairie at the sharp line of horizon between earth and sky encircling this place of circles within circles with the prehistoric cairn at its centre. ❈

these cairns may have served as burial sites to honour renowned tribal leaders. Some, altered over generations, probably served prehistoric ceremonial purposes, such as the one connected with long-past rain dances. Some may have marked the boundary of tribal territories, warning away potential attackers. Some are still occasionally used by Natives seeking spiritual guidance.

Sundial Medicine Wheel, located above the Oldman River on remote Sundial Hill, is a place of extraordinary simplicity. It is one of the most intact medicine wheels on the continent. From the high hill's crest there is nothing visible except hundreds of square kilometres of empty rolling grassland. The sky there is huge; the wind ceaseless. It hisses in the dry bunchgrass. It is possible that, as occurred at a number of other medicine wheels, the Natives fixed a vertical wooden pole amid the boulders of the 1.5-metre-high central cairn. During the day, its shadow would have swept the concentric circles exactly as would that of a sundial. But this is conjecture. There is no pole now . . . only the circles of stones, the rocky lichen-covered cairn, the wind, and the shadows of puffy prairie cumulus heading eastward toward Saskatchewan and the oblivion of evening.

The long grass bent to the bidding of the wind, then sprang up again.
"Who has seen the wind?" Fat shouted.
"Neither you nor I," returned Brian.

– W. O. MITCHELL, *WHO HAS SEEN THE WIND*

A WINDSTORM ALONG HIGHWAY 24, NEAR VULCAN, ALBERTA. It is a constant presence – an invisible force that defines the region, changes everything, penetrates the psyche, and rearranges the sky. The prairie wind is as specific to the Prairies as is the hiss of the ocean to the West Coast: a daily fact of life, a signature written in sound. Waves of wind roll across a field of ripening wheat, pushing piled-high clouds across the sky and hurrying their shadows across the land.

The wind never stops. Like earth, air, fire, and water, on the Prairies the wind is a fundamental element. It changes character, scent, and direction, but it never stops. The average wind speed in southern Alberta is 20 kilometres per hour, every day, every night, year-round. In the winter the northerly wind polishes the snow and makes minus-40-degree-Celsius days unbearable; in the summer the west wind tosses tumbleweed around, creates dust devils, stirs mosquitoes, and makes evenings bearable. It blows thunderstorms across the plains, twists itself into a tornado, carries away topsoil, drives cottonwood fluff through the air, plants seeds, riffles the yellowing canola. Farmers curse it and praise it. Children run with it on their way to

---

BUFFALO JUMPS: REMNANTS OF TRAGEDY

The hunt started several weeks before the bison kill. The tribe's Buffalo Woman performed ceremonies using her iniskims (ammonite fossils) to conjure the animals and to call them east from the Albertan foothills. Men repaired the drive lanes, marked by rock cairns that outline a V-shaped path soon to be filled with buffalo thundering toward an invisible cliff. Everyone gathered for the ritual blessing of the buffalo runners, respected adolescent males whose fathers once ran out across the prairie to find the bison the Buffalo Woman had located in her dreams. The runners became animals. They would wear the skins of wolves, coyotes, and buffalo; they would behave like them, call like them.

Finally the herds of buffalo would arrive in the mouth of the drive lanes. The hunters would then rush at the animals from behind, forcing them toward the cliff, still six kilometres away. Fires were lit amid shouting and the waving of buffalo hides. The bison, panicked by the smell of smoke and the screams of people, would run at 50 kilometres per hour over the 10-metre cliff. Those that didn't die in the fall would die from the spears and arrows waiting below. The final count would be at least 200, maybe 400 buffalo, enough for the coming winter. There would be horn for spoons, skin for

---

school, their jackets open like spread wings; returning home in the afternoon, they close their eyes against the grit it spits at them. The wind feels cleansing, bitter, punishing, tender. A force to be reckoned with, shaping everything that lives here, planting impermanence in those who have the Prairies in their bones. "The steady hand of the wind on his back," wrote W. O. Mitchell of one of his characters, "was the hand that moved the sky." ❧

Thousands of mating mosquitoes swirl like a whining tornado in the early-evening stillness. It is at times like this that residents of the Prairies pray for the intervention of wind. DANIEL WOOD

clothing and tents, and food – fresh meat that would be eaten at the jump or dried and pounded with chokecherries, Saskatoon berries, and fat to make pemmican. And there would be tongue for the Buffalo Woman.

There were once thousands of buffalo jumps on the plains of Alberta, Saskatchewan, North Dakota, and Montana; the most intact is Head-Smashed-In Buffalo Jump, 170 kilometres southwest of Calgary, where

archaeologist Dick Forbis and his associates dug from 1965 to 1972. They learned that the jump was regularly used for 5,700 years, until as recently as 1860. They estimated that 123,000 buffalo died there after stampeding through 30 different drive lanes marked by about 15,000 cairns. Despite the effectiveness of these Native buffalo jumps, 60 million buffalo lived on the plains at the time of the arrival of the first white settlers. By the end of the 19th century,

however, there were only 1,000 buffalo left in North America.

Says Forbis of the slaughter: "You can't blame the Indians for exterminating the buffalo. They'd been at it – hunting buffalo – for 10,000 years. I think there was, at least partially, a deliberate policy by the whites to destroy the buffalo herds as a way of conquering the Indians and taking away their food."

Turning and turning in the widening gyre
The falcon cannot hear the falconer;
Things fall apart; the centre cannot hold;
Mere anarchy is loosed upon the world ...

– WILLIAM BUTLER YEATS, "THE SECOND COMING"

Beverley

SUNRISE AT OLD WOMEN'S BUFFALO JUMP, CAYLEY, ALBERTA. I have never made eye contact with a bird before. This one, tawny grey and huge, sits like a harbinger of doom on a signpost at the intersection of two rural backroads and *stares* at us while we slow down, trying to choose between conflicting directions. Straight ahead? Or right? Its head turns and its gaze follows us as Daniel stops and backs up to have a closer look at it. Its eyes are unwavering, almost threatening. Then it flies to the right. We take this as an omen. The bird – we later learn it is a red-tailed hawk – has shown us the way to Old Women's Buffalo Jump.

But there is more than one hawk. Two circle above the cottonwoods, perch, and watch with huge eyes as we pitch our tent in the long grass of an abandoned farmyard. Between a half-collapsed chicken coop and a rusted-out pickup truck, a tire swing hangs like a noose. Curtains blow out the window of the dilapidated trailer behind us. In the distance coyotes bark. The place is eerie. The eroded coulee, where over the centuries thousands of buffalo and unknown numbers of Natives have died, is a five-minute walk from here. As the sun sets, the hawks again drift above us, crying ominously, and Daniel, trying to imitate their guttural sound, decides it is like the noise made by someone being strangled. This isn't what I want to hear. I sleep fitfully and wake in the darkness, startled by what I think are the voices of children playing, then dream of a woman with huge eyes clawing at me and crying out in a language I can't understand. I am relieved when I see the sky turning from black to pink above Old Women's Buffalo Jump. ❖

As dawn breaks above Squaw Coulee, mooing cattle wander up to the sandstone bluff where, for two millennia, Plains Indians drove buffalo to their deaths. Archaeologist Dick Forbis, now 73, decoded the myth and history of the site. DANIEL WOOD

Daniel

SUNRISE AT OLD WOMEN'S BUFFALO JUMP, CAYLEY, ALBERTA. We have come to this forlorn place because no one else does. It is a place doubly abandoned: first by 19th-century Blackfoot women because the buffalo had disappeared; second by archaeologist Dick Forbis, who spent 1958 here, unearthing centuries of human occupation and decoding the myths of the place. Today it is a place inhabited by ghosts. We have arisen before dawn, crossed a barbed-wire fence, and found a perch above Squaw Coulee, facing east. The sky is as

This huge glacial erratic, known as The Big Rock, is a memento mori from the Ice Age when 13 million square kilometres of Canada lay beneath a continent-wide icefield. DANIEL WOOD

THE OKOTOKS GLACIAL ERRATIC: THE STORY OF A WANDERING MONSTER

The landscape of the West bears the imprint of the 2,000-metre-thick Ice Age glaciers that scoured the land repeatedly and left in their wake evidence of their passage. The end of the last period of glaciation came abruptly and inexplicably 10,500 years ago when the Earth suddenly warmed and the ice melted. Soon, in succession, bacteria, lichens, plants, animals, and humans repopulated the wasteland, softening the edges of glaciation, but leaving its artifacts untouched. The U-shaped fjords of the B.C. coast, the hummocky moraine remnants south of Drumheller, Alberta, the myriad lakes of the Yukon, the long, 15-metre-high drumlin ridge southwest of Red Deer, Alberta – these and 10,000 other features attest to the glaciers' passing.

In a field eight kilometres west of Okotoks, Alberta, lies a unique memento of the Ice Age. The Big Rock, as it is locally known, is the world's largest glacial erratic, weighing in at an estimated 16,400 tonnes. The broken boulder is, in fact, part of the 500-kilometre-long Foothills Glacial Train, a line of rocky debris that stretches from its source at Mount Edith Cavell near Jasper, Alberta, to the U.S. border. Glaciologists now know that 18,000 years ago a massive landslide deposited a load of pebbly quartzite on the surface of a passing Ice Age glacier. Over the passing millennia the landslide debris was borne southeastward, along with hundreds of other gargantuan boulders, coming to a halt with the gradual melting of the ice. The 41-metre-long, 18-metre-wide, nine-metre-high Big Rock sits in an Okotoks field, a mute reminder of the West's recent geologic past.

pale as tears. The creek below is shrouded in a ropy mist that conceals the water but not the burbling. The hawks of the night before have ceased their circling and crying, the coyotes their yipping.

In 1957 a flash flood exposed thousands of bleached buffalo bones below the 10-metre-high sandstone bluff where we now sit. Forbis, then 33, decided to utilize this odd revelation to do his first serious archaeological work. He soon learned that Blackfoot myths described the site as an old buffalo jump, a cliff – like thousands of others in the West – used by Natives to drive herds of plains buffalo to their death. This site was, however, unique because, according to myth, unlike all the others, it was controlled by women. Forbis began digging. It was, at it often is in archaeology, hot, boring, backbreaking labour. Working downward with shovels, shoring up the ever-deepening pit walls with two-by-fours, Forbis and his crew descended into the past. Some layers were full of bone, hair, and decomposing buffalo hide. Some were white with the ashes of burnt bone. Some contained exquisite fluted and notched projectile points, rounded scrapers, and heavy choppers, the shapes of which indicated their age. "I wondered if it would ever end," Forbis says today of the treasures he kept finding. At 6.5 metres the diggers hit groundwater, but by then Forbis had uncovered 2,000 years of continuous human usage at the buffalo jump on Squaw Creek.

He could see in the strata when bows and arrows were first introduced to the Plains Indians around 600 A.D. and where, more than a millennium later, the horse appeared, displacing the young buffalo runners who had previously listened to the prophecies of Buffalo Woman and had chased the herds off this cliff. In the end, he filled the hole, reburying the past. The past is a place, he realized in the decades ahead, that is forever unreachable. "I'd like to have a time machine," Forbis says wistfully of his life's work, "and be able to go back and . . . and *live* with the people who were living then – hear their songs, hear their stories, their sad lives and happy lives. But you can't get that out of archaeology. We can only catch the briefest glimpses of the tribes of the Plains."

The sun's first rays shoot from the silhouetted black bluffs across Squaw Coulee like the power rays emanating from the heads of the petroglyph shamans carved into the sandstone at Writing-on-Stone not far to the south. Nearer, just off to my left, Beverley is quietly humming a familiar melody: "Here Comes the Sun." 🏮

FOLLOWING PAGES The wildly eroded badlands of south-central Alberta contain the world's best collection of dinosaur bones. GREIF-CZOLOWSKI PHOTOGRAPHY

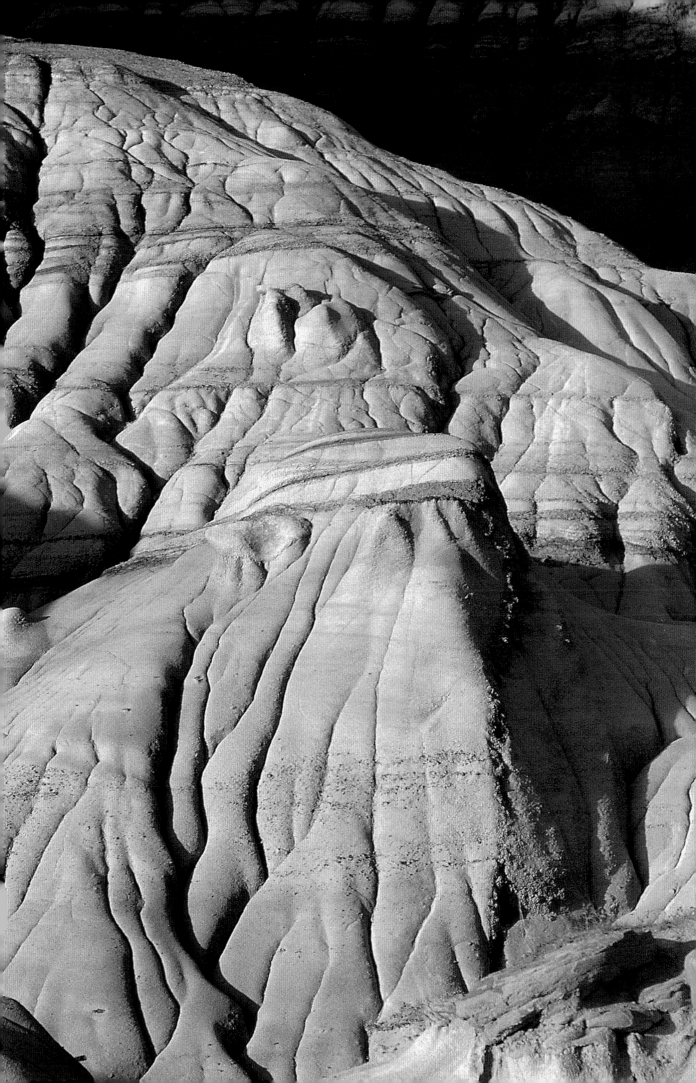

*What a trifling difference must often determine
which shall survive and which shall perish.*

– CHARLES DARWIN

Daniel

DINOSAUR HUNTING OUTSIDE DRUMHELLER, ALBERTA.
Phil Currie, 48, is a man accustomed to seeing bones
where others see dirt. Walking the eroded coulees above
the Red Deer River near Drumheller, Alberta, with his hyperac-
tive sheltie named Seven, the lanky, soft-spoken palaeontologist
looks down and says to me: "A bone." Removing a small yellow-
handled awl from his hip pack, he crouches and gently pries free
a shiny five-centimetre tyrannosaur tooth. Not much farther on
he spots the metre-long leg bone of a duckbilled dinosaur. From
its state of disintegration, he estimates that it has lain exposed to
summer heat and prairie cold for several years. It is crumbling,
beyond saving. Seven sniffs the bone and Currie and I laugh at
the incongruity: the bone is bigger than the dog.

Like most experts we have met on our travels, Currie is
obsessed. Ever since the day in 1955 when he dumped some Rice
Krispies into a bowl and found the promised plastic dinosaur –
he still has that toy – he has been a man consumed by dinosaurs:
their size, power, ferocity, and evolutionary history. This absorp-
tion has carried him on fossil digs around the world, but of
the badlands that stretch southward from Drumheller past
Alberta's Dinosaur Provincial Park to the U.S. border he says:
"It's an embarrassment of riches. It's the best in the world. At
so many dinosaur sites you get a few scraps of bone. Here, you
pick and choose."

The explanation for this extraordinary fossil abundance
requires a brief recounting of the region's geologic history.
Seventy-five million years ago much of Alberta was a vast flood-
plain cut by meandering rivers that flowed into the warm
Bearpaw Sea to the east. The climate was Caribbean. Of the
planet's 300 known species of dinosaur, 35 lived here, including
the rhinolike ankylsaurs, the tube-headed hadrosaurs, and their
nemesis, the nine-metre-long tyrannosaurs. Some were buried
and preserved singly; some ended up in mass bone beds containing hundreds of fossilized creatures. The recent Pleistocene
glaciation strip-mined the overburdened earth so that today, as
erosion cuts into the coulees of central Alberta, at least six new
dinosaur bodies and tens of thousands of fragments are revealed
each year. Just south of here Currie has excavated the nests (full
of grapefruit-sized fossil eggs) of 10-metre-long duckbilled

dinosaurs, while his associates have found part of a flying pterosaur with a wingspan of 13 metres.

As I follow Currie, I am caught up in his compulsion, his endless scanning of the eroded and layered badlands as he seeks evidence of the Age of Dinosaurs. Sometimes he toes a bit of mineralized bone and moves on without stopping; sometimes he stoops and reads the fossil, naming a creature that died 70 million years ago. I find myself wishing I had his fluency in the language of bones. The earth speaks to him; I want it to speak to me. ▦

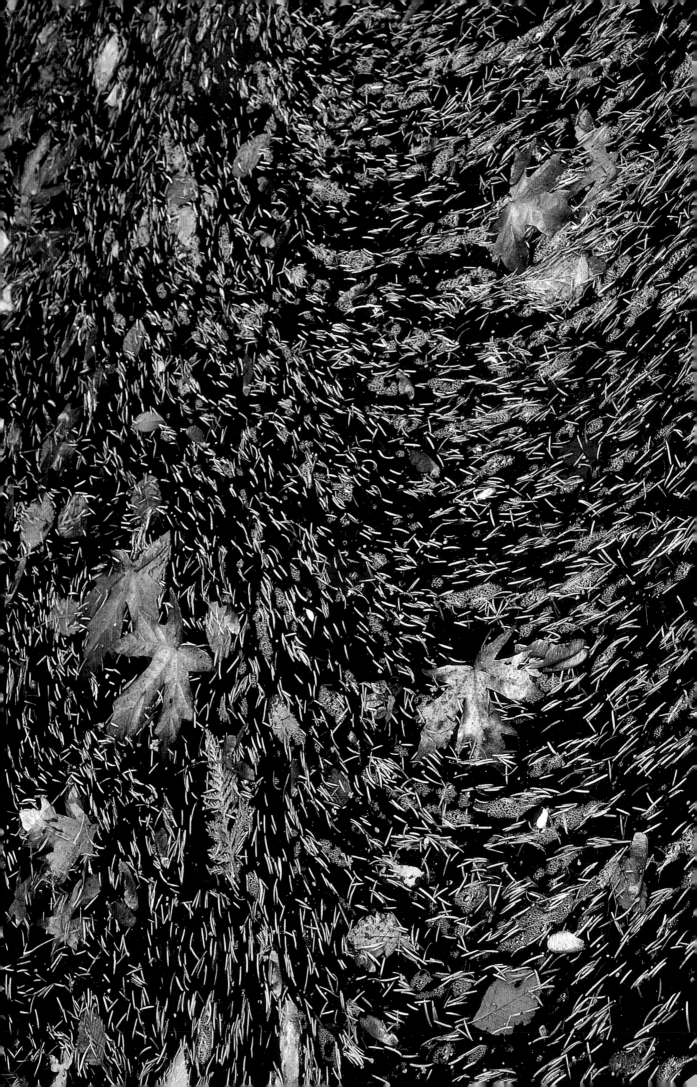

V   TRAVELLERS AND INTRUDERS:

NORTHERN ALBERTA AND BRITISH COLUMBIA'S
PEACE RIVER REGION

Some say the world
will end in fire:
Some say in ice.

– ROBERT FROST, "FIRE AND ICE".

Daniel

TORNADO-CHASING AT EVERGREEN MOBILE HOME PARK OUTSIDE EDMONTON, ALBERTA. There are always two sides to a story and this is no exception: a tornado looks different from the inside than it does from the outside. I have knocked on the door of 22 Evergreen Avenue in Evergreen Mobile Home Park northeast of Edmonton and, after explaining my purpose to Marilyn and Phil Demers, am invited to sit on the couch. On the muggy afternoon of July 31, 1987, while sitting in precisely the same spot I now occupy, the couple had watched the sky outside turn an otherworldly yellow-green. They had seen plenty of prairie thunderstorms but never, they tell me, one like this. Fierce gusts of wind drove dust and leaves sideways past their windows and hail pummelled their mobile home. Then the power went out. As Marilyn watched, a large object – a human being – flew past the living room window, moving horizontally, three metres off the ground. Then came the sound. "It was like a freight train," says Marilyn, struggling to describe the disaster. "It was like jets' engines, explosions, thunder – all together. It was tremendous! It was incredible! Then . . . I flew!" Caught in the wreckage of her exploding home, she looked up into the tornado's funnel and saw debris, including her neighbour's roof, lifting skyward. She told herself: "This is the end of the world."

For the Demerses it wasn't the end. But for 15 others who lived on Evergreen Avenue it was.

Dennis Dudley, 32, only knows cyclones from the outside, but in his role as southern Alberta's severe-weather meteorologist and a member of the tornado-chasing Fighting Prairie Weather Dogs, he is thrilled by the prospect of a Close Encounter of the Worst Kind. He knows that 20 or so twisters hit Alberta each year. Most are harmless. Once every five years, however, one of these assumes an F4 or F5 rating on the Fujita scale: winds from 331 to 509 kilometres an hour. He knows what can happen then. Dudley was working at Edmonton's Weather Centre on July 31, 1987, watching the radar and the sky. The day, like the previous days, was almost unbearable: hot and very humid. Dudley knew that a cold front was moving in from the Rockies and that this mixture, the humid prairie air and the cold mountain air, was a recipe for severe weather. A line of thunderstorms, moving northeastward, showed on the radar. As he studied the darkening sky outside, secretly hoping he would see a tornado, a thin grey ropelike funnel descended from the advancing storm front, still 30 kilometres away. The funnel touched the ground, grew dark, and gradually expanded

PAGE 94 These fallen evergreen needles, along with red alder and maple leaves, float on an autumnal, bubble-filled Vancouver Island stream.
TIM FITZHARRIS/MASTERFILE

OPPOSITE PAGE A meteorological map of Alberta's severest weather events, including, on average, 20 annual tornados, centres on Stettler, east of Red Deer. As Edmonton's Marilyn and Phil Demers know, when a nightmarish F4 tornado hits, only a few survive. CLAUDE LAVOIE/FIRST LIGHT

to a kilometre in width. Dudley couldn't understand why a tremendous flock of birds was circling the approaching cyclone. Then it hit him: it wasn't birds at all; it was debris, rooftops, trees, and cars – flying.

By the time the F4 tornado had cut a 40-kilometre path through Edmonton's eastern suburbs almost an hour had passed and 27 people had died. This single storm produced an estimated 30,000 lightning strikes, hail the size of softballs, and winds in excess of 400 kilometres an hour. As Dudley recounts the events to us, he sits in his office beneath an enlarged news photo of the tornado. The awe and excitement in his voice are palpable. I find myself envious. The tornado gave him an obsession, a purpose. He had seen the moving hand of God, writing in cursive script the fate of those in the tornado's path. "It's almost like a modern-day nightmare – these monsters," he says of prairie cyclones. "They're almost too unbelievable to imagine. They're the last frontier in meteorology. There are still many, many more questions than answers about tornadoes. They develop out of thin air . . . and disappear just as quick." 🏛

FUJITA SCALE OF CYCLONIC WINDS

▸ F0 (64-115 KILOMETRES PER HOUR): *Some roof shingles and siding removed and tree branches broken. Garden furniture blown around.*

▸ F1 (116-179 KILOMETRES PER HOUR): *Roofing stripped from buildings, hydroelectric transmission towers and some trees knocked down, cottages pushed off foundations.*

▸ F2 (180-251 KILOMETRES PER HOUR): *Structural failure of roofs and porches, barns demolished, unanchored buildings rolled over, farm equipment carried short distances. Trees uprooted. Impact damage from flying missiles.*

▸ F3 (252-330 KILOMETRES PER HOUR): *Extensive damage to frame houses, with two-story houses moved from foundations. Tombstones blown over. Trailers and automobiles hurled through air.*

▸ F4 (331-416 KILOMETRES PER HOUR): *Two-story brick houses almost completely destroyed. Automobiles, mobile homes, and heavy farm equipment carried long distances through the air. Extensive structural damage to industrial buildings.*

▸ F5 (417-509 KILOMETRES PER HOUR): *Total destruction; little remains intact.*

I was of three minds,
Like a tree
In which there are three blackbirds.

– WALLACE STEVENS, "THIRTEEN WAYS OF LOOKING AT A BLACKBIRD"

Beverley

BETWEEN A ROCK AND A HARD PLACE AT ELK ISLAND NATIONAL PARK, EAST OF EDMONTON. Daniel seems remarkably calm as he descends the hill, given two important facts: (1) we are approaching a couple of 1,000-kilogram animals that stand two metres at the shoulder; (2) we are separated from them by only a clump of small aspen. Beneath the glowing early-evening sky, the buffalo are grazing, 30 metres from us now, beside a marshy lake.

The plains bison are something of an anachronism, belonging to a time when the grasses they feed on covered the North American prairie. Now about 700 live in this fenced, 195-square-kilometre park, their only natural habitat in Canada; 7,000 live on Alberta ranches, destined to become steak or hamburger. (Just 125 years ago, almost *10,000 times* as many plains bison – 60 million – roamed the North American grasslands.) As Wes Olsen, an Elk Island bison expert, put it, "There's no place for the plains bison. The grasslands are mostly owned or fenced or gone."

The bison look up at us, not with alarm, but with a nonchalance that matches Daniel's. Then a movement at the bottom of the hill catches my eye. A moose – at 350 kilograms, the largest member of the deer family – is loping through the trees. She sees me as I see her. She stops, ears on alert to make up for her poor eyesight. And then her calf, gangly and ridiculously long-legged, appears, following her tentatively. The mother, to my astonishment, doesn't turn and run away but, instead, walks directly toward me. Her calf follows. They are 60 metres from me . . . now 45 . . . now 30. Crouched in the knee-high grass, I glance over my shoulder at Daniel to make sure he is aware of the two moose and see, beyond him, the steaming breath coming from the nostrils of the bison. Daniel is, in fact, glancing over *his* shoulder trying to reconcile the odd situation. We are outflanked, caught in a wildlife sandwich. The mother moose comes still closer and stops 15 metres from me. She studies me, then lowers her head to graze, and the calf begins to nurse. I cannot believe it; I don't know which way to look.

We stay there, silently, for a long time – Daniel and I, the two bison, and the moose and her calf – long enough for the early-evening shadows to stretch toward night. And all I can think is: this is amazing. ❧

THE UPSIDE-DOWN FLOWER POTS ON THE CLEARWATER RIVER

On the Alberta-Saskatchewan border east of Fort McMurray the river has eroded the grey-brown rock into strange shapes that look like inverted flower pots. This series of seldom-seen towers, 10 to 15 metres high and sprouting spruce trees from their tops, is evidence of the area's dolomitic karst topography. Like sections of north-central Vancouver Island, karst regions are noted for their caves, spires, and contorted rock forms.

Kelp and barnacles are a study in intertidal adaptation. No ecological zone demands the sheer tenacity that coastal wave zones dictate. This could be a handicap for sexual reproduction, but not for barnacles.
GREIF-CZOLOWSKI PHOTOGRAPHY

TRAVELLING TREES, BARNACLE SEX, AND OTHER CURIOUS PHENOMENA

▸ Trees move. As the climate gets warmer, trees get more sexually active, producing more pollen and cones. Six thousand years ago, when the planet was suddenly much warmer, by 3.5 to 4.5 degrees Celsius, the tree line in Canada's Arctic moved northward at a rate of 100 metres per year. By the end of that surge, the northern spruce forest occu-

pied 400 kilometres of what is now tundra. With global warming, this is certain to occur again.

▸ A typical Alberta day in early summer contains 5,000 lightning strikes. A bad day – or good, if you happen to like watching prairie thunderstorms – contains 50,000 lightning strikes.

▸ One of the fundamental facts of life for a barnacle is that it is stuck. The glue that attaches it to surf-side rocks prevents it

At the height of the annual spring runoff (May to mid-July), the mouth of British Columbia's Fraser River carries 15,000 cubic metres of water seaward per second; in midwinter the flow is reduced to a mere 400 cubic metres per second.

The earth moves, too. Mountains erode at the rate of a half millimetre per year. The mountains of the West Coast are, curiously, rising at about the same rate. The continents are drifting, on average, about two centimetres per year, the same speed at which human fingernails grow. Landslides can move at nearly 100 kilometres per hour.

An adult porcupine has about 30,000 quills.

A gnat beats its five-millimetre-long wings approximately 500 flaps per second. A hummingbird beats its six-centimetre-long wings approximately 50 wing beats per second. A mute swan's 70-centimetre-long wings flap a sedate 1.5 beats per second.

Canada's most bizarre animal is probably the mountain beaver of extreme southwestern British Columbia. Despite its name, it is not a beaver. It is the only living descendant of the Earth's first rodent and is, thus, a living fossil. It spends much of its life underground, tunnelling and eating the roots of plants.

One of the most lethal plants in this region is poison hemlock, a common tall white-flowered member of the carrot family. It is the juices of this plant, not those of the hemlock tree, that were used to kill Socrates. The mushroom known as *Amanita pantherina,* a brownish version of the more famous red-capped *Amanita muscaria,* is the region's deadliest fungus.

Under the tectonic pressure in the subduction zone off Vancouver Island's west coast, the southern region of the island is being both pushed toward the B.C. mainland and shoved upward seven millimetres each year. It has been 300 years since the last major quake here. When another great subduction earthquake occurs and the built-up pressure of three centuries is released, Vancouver Island will suddenly move (300 x 7 milli-metres equals 2,100 millimetres) 2.1 metres.

As every backcountry traveller knows, bears don't eat berries, they inhale them. Their blackish scat often demonstrates this. Research shows that enzymes in a bear's stomach strip the hulls off certain seeds, allowing the plant to germinate faster than it would otherwise. Chokecherries reproduce three times as fast and dogwoods seven times as fast if their seeds pass through a bear on their way to the soil.

from meeting sexual partners. To overcome this handicap, the barnacle needs a, well . . . long appendage. The penis of a barnacle is 20 times as long as its body. This appendage is pushed out of the barnacle's open orifice and into that of a neighbour. Since barnacles are hermaphroditic, any opening will do.

One large cedar of the Pacific Northwest has an estimated 70 million needles.

The threatened wood bison, a larger and darker relative of the plains buffalo, survives in small wild herds in Alberta's far north and in a smaller fenced herd east of Edmonton. GRAHAM OSBORNE

ENDANGERED SPECIES: APOCALYPSE NOW

Of the 274 highly endangered species in Canada, not to mention the hundreds more that are rare or threatened, the 1.5-metre-tall whooping crane is the one that has become the emblem of survival against long odds. In 1941 there were exactly 21 on Earth – a total of five breeding pairs plus 11 young. Of these, 16 migrated annually to Wood Buffalo National Park on the Alberta-Northwest Territories border. At latest count the whooping crane population in the park numbered 157 plus 30 or so chicks. Sighting one whooping crane, an extraordinary rarity in and of itself, is a moving reminder both of nature's tenuousness and of its tenacity. Says Brian Johns, a Saskatchewan-based whooping crane expert, "Every time I see one, even now, I get excited because I know how few there are."

Across the Canadian West a number of endangered and threatened species are, like the whooping crane, making comebacks against centuries of habitat loss and human predation. But on a planetary scale these glimpses of hope are rare. Worldwide, 5,205 different species, including one-quarter of all mammals and 10 percent of all birds, face imminent extinction. So any and every victory over the spectre of annihilation in the West – examples include the grey whale, the plains bison, the peregrine falcon – means the ominous worldwide trend threatening thousands of species has, in some tiny way, been mitigated by people who hope one day to see a family of whooping cranes overhead.

Here are just a few western creatures – there are scores more endangered plants, molluscs, insects, and fungi – that live on the cusp of oblivion:

- The sharp-tailed snake of Pender Island, British Columbia, and the western hognose snake of southern Alberta are endangered by habitat loss.

- The Vancouver Island marmot, one of the country's rarest mammals, lives in six isolated subalpine colonies. Their population has recently decreased to 200.

- The population of the northern leopard frog, once the most common frog species in North America, is in steep decline. No one knows why. Pockets of them are found in the wetlands of southern Alberta.

- The Nooksack dace, a small fish found in British Columbia's Fraser Valley, may be extinct in Canada within a few years.

- The burrowing owl of the Alberta and B.C. grasslands – like its endangered relative, the spotted owl of the B.C. rainforest – faces extinction through habitat loss. There are currently about 1,000 breeding pairs of the tiny owls in Alberta and even fewer pairs in British Columbia's Okanagan Valley.

- The 30-centimetre-long brownish-purple Pacific giant salamander is threatened by the loss of its habitat near Chilliwack Lake east of Vancouver. It is so hard to find that scientists believe it may already be extinct in Canada.

- The swift fox of southeastern Alberta once numbered zero but, since the release of American animals, there are now about 250 in the region.

- The gregarious right whale (it was considered "right" for killing) numbers just 200 off the B.C. coast and has not recovered despite over 50 years of protection.

The 1.5-metre-tall whooping crane, once common across western North America, is one of the planet's rarest creatures. But it has made a dramatic comeback since 1941, increasing its population almost ninefold to about 187 birds. BRIAN MILNE/FIRST LIGHT

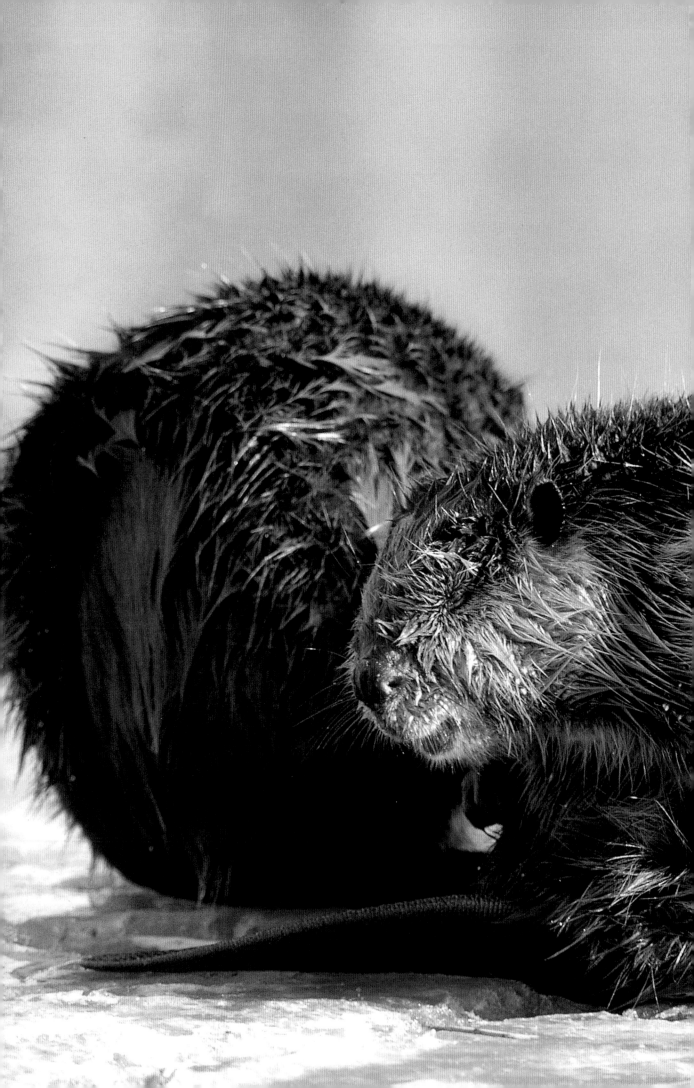

Daniel

TWILIGHT AT ELK ISLAND'S BEAVER POND. Until this moment the only things we have heard about beavers have been bad. They are blocking irrigation ditches, people said. They are destroying prairie windbreaks, killing valuable timber, and making a general nuisance of themselves across the West. It sounded as though Canada's national symbol, spreading rapidly into its old haunts after two centuries of extermination, was becoming a pest. But here in the last minutes of dusk, balanced precariously on a slime-covered fallen log above a series of slimy half-metre-deep beaver canals and an even more slimy mosquito-infested marsh, what we hear — extraordinarily close — is an odd *crunch-crunch-crunch*. It sounds as though someone with poor manners were engaged in the open-mouthed chewing of old bubble gum. Behind me, Beverley inching nearer; ahead of me, a beaver (I am pretty sure) chewing; below me, mud of an indeterminate depth. Beverley and I exchange beaver-overbite expressions and inch further along the log. We freeze.

Below us now, just five metres distant, a glistening flat-backed beaver is whittling the end of an alder branch. It is . . . okay, I'll say it: cute. Poised like a pair of uneasy tightrope walkers above the muddy sluiceway, we are unprepared for what happens next. The beaver suddenly dives and whacks the water with its leathery, 30-centimetre-long tail. *Crack!* It seems as loud as a gunshot. My reflexes launch me backward, teetering and tottering. *Whoooooa! Mega-mud below!* Beverley grabs me. *We* now teeter, a couple of drunks intoxicated by adrenaline. By the time we have recovered our balance and our nervous giggles have subsided, the beaver has reappeared and is studying us, trying, it seems, to assess our intentions. Beyond it other beavers silently ferry sticks to the nearby two-metre-high lodge, home to 10 or so creatures. The pond's surface is now the colour of pewter; the silhouetted beavers are black. The animal below us recommences its noisy ruminations.

Despite the complaints we have heard about the West's resurgent beaver population, I find myself rooting for the buck-toothed rodent. After all, the Plains Indians believed that humankind was formed from clay that had been brought up from the bottom of a pond by a beaver. And the animal has survived, although barely, almost 500 years of being turned into hats. So each adult beaver cuts down, on average, 216 trees, mostly alder, a year. (A 20-centimetre-wide tree can be toppled by a beaver in 15 minutes.) So beaver dams sometimes cause minor flooding. (The largest dam ever recorded was a three-

PREVIOUS PAGES These three beavers, two parents and their kit, rest on the midwinter ice of Alberta's Bow River. As the demand for pelts has decreased, the beaver has reestablished itself across the Prairies. WAYNE WEGNER/ FIRST LIGHT

metre-high, 1,500-metre-long monstrosity across the Bow River in Saskatchewan.) As we watch the busy Brueghelesque scene before us, I am filled with a sense of delight. The only sound here at the pond's edge is that of chewing. The beaver eyes us but doesn't flee. It seems to know that, after half a millennium, time is on its side. ▦

Where the telescope ends, the microscope begins.

– VICTOR HUGO, *LES MISÉRABLES*

Beverley

LOOKING FOR CARNIVOROUS PLANTS IN WAGNER BOG WEST OF EDMONTON. As we start walking, I decide two things: first, not to tell Daniel that a gadzillion representatives of this region's 30 species of mosquitoes have turned his blue jeans black; second, not to look at my own legs. Naturalist Alice Hendry, 55, her grey half-metre-long braid trailing down from under her Tilley hat, says, "They sure are pesky. But this is their place, and we're the visitors." Daniel slathers himself with DEET, I pull my sleeves down over my hands, and we head into the black spruce and Labrador tea. It is dry underfoot, but it won't be for long: we are headed for mud.

The range of miniature ecosystems crammed into this 129-hectare calcium carbonate-rich marl swamp is enormous. About one-third of all Alberta's plant species live here, including five types of carnivorous plants. Those who love this bog see beauty where others see only pond slime, moss, bugs, and plants you can't see without getting down on your knees.

THE POLLEN STORMS OF THE BOREAL FORESTS

In late June the northern forests grow hot. The heat rises. Westerly winds blow. The lodgepole pines sway. And each tiny male cone on these pines releases an explosion of microscopic airborne sperm – 30 million from a single tree – that coalesce with the pollen from millions of other trees, forming a dense sulphur-coloured cloud. Individually just 30 to 50 microns in diameter (one micron equals one-thousandth of a millimetre), the grains create a wind-propelled pollen storm. Seen from an airplane or a ridge top, these huge and dense clouds fill valleys and assume the appearance of smoke from a forest fire. The clouds sweep eastward, obscuring treetops and coating every hectare, every bush, every pond with a thick yellow veneer.

Alberta palynologist (pollen expert) Charlie Schweger reports that most of the pollen from Canada's boreal pine, spruce, and fir forests falls within a few hundred metres of its source. But the wind always lifts some of this pollen into the jet stream, with the result that it can be used in the dating of buried strata within Greenland's ice cap, 6,000 kilometres distant.

As we walk, the ground becomes increasingly spongy underfoot. Daniel jumps up and down a couple of times and visible waves move out across the earth's surface, making it look as though he had been bouncing on a waterbed. Because of the waterlogged anaerobic conditions here, dead plants don't decay but build up to form an organic substratum of peat. Soon we are following Hendry's footsteps undeviatingly through the fen, where a misplaced step could land us in waist-deep muck. Our rubber boots are just high enough to keep out the acidic water and just tight enough to resist the suctioning, downward pull of almost 5,000 years of peat.

When I heard there were orchids here, I hadn't envisioned needing a magnifying glass to see them. We are all on our knees, searching for a green needle in a green haystack. The rare bog-adder's-mouth orchid, one of 15 orchid species found here, is not like those that make it into Hawaiian leis. The entire plant is four centimetres high; the flower is a half millimetre across and 1.5 millimetres long. They are astounding. Perfect orchids but miniscule, almost invisible, challenging my mind to adjust to a new scale, a new way of seeing, a new world.

Bug-encircled and mud-covered, we begin searching for tiny marsh-dwelling carnivorous sundews. They eat insects but not, unfortunately, mosquitoes. Instead of kneeling in the muck to study them, Daniel points his binoculars down and steps back, focusing at the closest distance. He hands me his binoculars and there they are at my feet: lime-green jewel-like pincushions framed by glistening crimson rays, each flower half the size of my little fingernail. The miniscule hairs surrounding each sundew end in sticky crystal pearls. The strange plants look like a child's painting of the sun. To me they are exquisite miniatures; to unwary insects, death.

"The big things are easy to spot. They reach out and punch you," says Hendry, who kneels again and again to inspect some bog-hugging terrestrial or pond-edge aquatic plant. "The small things, though . . . they're quiet and contemplative." ❊

The crimson sticky-tipped hairs radiating off these tiny sundews look like the "power lines" encircling the heads of shamanistic petroglyph figures of the West. The hairs actually capture insects which, when consumed by the carnivorous plant, provide nitrogen. IAN LANE

I'll meet you on the dark side of the moon.

– PINK FLOYD, "DARK SIDE OF THE MOON"

Beverley

ON HIGHWAY 34 EAST OF GRANDE PRAIRIE, ALBERTA.
I have picked up three rolls of pictures that I had taken
in this region and, until I see the results, had not been
aware that I had been quenching a thirst – a thirst for the landscape that was implanted in my bones by my Prairie birth. It is, I
see from my photos, a thirst for sky, for what Emerson calls "the
daily bread of the eyes." As Saskatchewan-based photographer
Courtenay Milne once told me, "The sky means freedom. You
grow up with all that space around you and you feel you can
explore. You're lured over the next horizon. It makes adventur-

DISCOVERING THE UNMAPPED PLACE CALLED TERRA INCOGNITA

Soil, like faith, is the substance of things hoped for, the evidence of things not seen.

– FIRMAN E. BEAR, *EARTH: THE STUFF OF LIFE*

A handful of soil scooped from the earth outside, say, Mayerthorpe, Alberta, tells an elaborate story, although to understand it requires fluency in the arcane language of Terra Incognita. That handful of soil speaks of time and change and the rejuvenative power of nature. It can be perceived as an antidote to end-of-millennium hand-wringing. During the past two million years, Canada has four times been buried by massive continent-wide glaciers. The last Ice Age ended 10,500 years ago. Until the ice withdrew, the land was not merely clearcut and strip-mined, it was scoured to bedrock. The dirt dis-

appeared. Organic life ceased.

That handful of Alberta soil began to form as the melting ice and the Earth's natural acids worked on pulverized granitic bedrock, slowly releasing potassium from the feldspar, iron and magnesium from the biotite, and calcium from the hornblende. Microbes infiltrated the mineral-rich soil and morainal clays left by the glaciers. Plants and animals soon followed. At a rate of five centimetres of soil every thousand years the bedrock became covered with a veneer of organic dirt. Within 5,000 years, a nanosecond in geologic time, all that had been previously erased by the Ice Age had returned.

To pause and reflect on a seemingly inanimate handful of dirt – any handful will do – can provoke the realization that it contains a constellation as complex as an entire galaxy. That single handful contains, in fact,

more than 100 billion tiny animals: white millipedes, brownish mites, and buff-coloured springtails ceaselessly wander about looking for food, while billions of microscopic protozoa, like visions out of Kafka's worst nightmares, pursue their prey with pseudopods and flagella. But it is not just the unseen organic world that bears consideration. The 17 inorganic elements found in the soil are the same 17 elements from which comes all life. In fact, when a human body is cremated, the gases acquired through breathing and eating – oxygen, nitrogen, and hydrogen – are driven off. The five percent that remains – the powdery greyish ashes destined for the urn – are the 14 minerals that began as granite at the end of the Ice Age. Earth to earth, ashes to ashes, dust to dust.

ers of us. It makes us independent." The road stretches ahead and behind us through endless brilliant yellow canola fields, linking one edge of the sky with the other.

It was near here, I tell Daniel, that my parents and I, driving to Saskatchewan, stopped a few years ago because we couldn't keep moving while the sky seemed to be split into two halves – the moon claiming the eastern, the sun the western – with the road we were travelling being a black line connecting them. On the ground was the blue-white of midwinter dusk. But in the sky! To the right a full moon so huge it looked as if it wouldn't be able to lift off the horizon was presiding over a mauve twilight; to the left, directly opposite the moon, the sun was setting in an inferno of orange, streaking the western sky with fuchsia.

The sky is the recipient of prayers; home of the Christian God, the Native Thunderbird, angels; provider of sun and rain, calendar and clock; and backdrop for celestial displays like the meteor explosion that occurred over Bruderheim, 65 kilometres northeast of Edmonton, on March 4, 1960. The night sky was suddenly lit up by a ball of fire – the largest meteor crash ever to be observed in Canada. Witnesses described an intense blue-white light dripping orange sparks and an enormous explosion. Sound waves shook the foundations of homes in a 5,000-square-kilometre area of central Alberta. In total, over 300 kilograms of stone and iron poured down in shattered boulders, some weighing more than 30 kilograms. Something to tell the grandchildren; something by which to mark time; something either to wish on or to fear. ❖

In this watery optical illusion on British Columbia's Muchalat Lake, a reflected ridge and portion of sky assume the shape of a landscape that doesn't exist. AL HARVEY

STEEN RIVER METEOR CRATER: GHOST OF AN APOCALYPSE

Today there is no sign of the crater or the meteor that made it. Time has erased the evidence. That the crater had once existed in the spruce- and muskeg-covered Cameron Hills west of Steen River in Alberta's northwest corner was discovered by a seismic crew looking for oil. They found a crustal anomaly, a buried depression, 25 kilometres across and an estimated 100 million years old.

Geophysicists now know that a gargantuan meteor struck the Earth here, creating a firestorm that likely incinerated everything within 100 kilometres and plunged the entire planet into prolonged darkness. The explosion, were it to occur now, would be equivalent to the simultaneous detonation of the globe's entire nuclear arsenal. Human life would probably cease. In recent years geophysicists have found that these so-called "Apollo Events" happen far more often than was previ-

ously thought. Once every few million years, the planet is the target of an earth-shattering comet or meteor strike. On average, five major new meteor craters are found annually somewhere on Earth. The total number of known meteor craters is 155; of these, 26 are in Canada. Highway 35, a desolate road that runs parallel to the Hay River as it flows northward through Alberta, passes an unmarked place where once occurred one of the world's greatest catastrophes.

FIRE AND THE PHOENIX IN THE BOREAL FOREST

Anyone who has ever stood close to an out-of-control crown fire, and 49-year-old Alberta fire protection officer Bruce Mac-Gregor is one, knows about hell. The smoke is overwhelming, suffocating. The forest roars like a hurricane. Flames soar 100 metres skyward from the tops of hundreds of incandescent trees, breaking free of the topmost branches and rising upward, on convection currents, in the form of gaseous orange-brown fire-balls. The oxygen itself, sucked into the inferno, drains from the air. "It's nature out of control," says MacGregor. "It's . . . I guess the word is amazing."

His region in the province's northeast corner can, during severe weather, receive 15,000 lightning strikes on a single night. Dozens of fires may erupt simultaneously. Every once in a great while, when the conditions are right, a fire can go berserk. This happened once during MacGregor's 30 years of fighting fires. At 6:00 p.m. on May 28, 1995, a small fire, fed on warm winds, tinder-dry cari-bou moss, and parched black spruce, erupted in front of him. It looked like a thermonuclear explosion. He and his fire-fighting crew fled. Within six hours the crown fire had raced 32 kilometres and, before it was extinguished, the Maryanna Lakes Fire had burned 48 days and consumed 133,000 hectares of boreal forest.

It has only been in the past two decades that fire, like other natural "predators," has come to be viewed as something to protect rather than as some-thing to suppress. Fire is now seen as a necessary part of nature's cycles. Unlike logging, which removes the nutrients from a forest forever, fire opens the earth to sunlight, returns the tree-trapped nutrients to the soil, fosters the growth of flow-ers and low bushes, and pro-vides grazing habitat for ungulates. From this long-range perspective, fire has the trans-forming capacity of the phoenix, a mythical peacocklike bird that arises from the ashes of its own destruction.

Fires like this may burn through the jack pine and black spruce of Alberta's boreal forests for weeks. Today fire is increasingly seen as an integral part of wood-lands' natural cycle.

MANLEY FREDLUND

BONES AND STONES: EARLIEST HUMANS IN THE WEST

To understand how Neolithic nomads came to British Columbia's Charlie Lake Cave 11,500 years ago, one needs to picture the final stages of North America's last Ice Age. Fifteen thousand or so years ago Siberian hunters occupied the ice-free northern Yukon. Mammoth bones, dating from that time and showing cut marks from human flensing, have been found within the Yukon's remote and northerly Bluefish Cave. This is the earliest certifiable evidence of humans in the Americas. Although thick and impenetrable ice covered most of the land to the south, a few scattered islands and peninsulas along the Alaska-B.C. coast remained unglaciated. Leapfrogging along these glacial refugia, early humans finally arrived south of the continental ice, swept inland, and soon encountered the massive bison herds of the northern plains. As the ice gradually retreated and the Alberta grasslands spread, the bison, closely pursued by nomadic hunters, moved northward. Eleven thousand eight hundred years ago, as research shows, the hunters were camping beside Vermilion Lakes in Alberta's Banff National Park, the oldest human site in that province. Continuing northward, still following the buffalo, the nomads found and utilized the seven-metre-long, five-metre-wide cliffside cave (it is still there) above Charlie Lake, 16 kilometres north of Fort St. John.

During three recent summers, archaeologists Knut Fladmark and Jonathan Driver, along with their crews, have dug the cave's mouth, gradually excavating a five-metre-deep pit. Working in teams, three scraping away the dirt within the hole and three more screening it for artifacts, the scientists collected several thousand human-related objects: stone chips for tool-making, smashed animal bones, chopping and cutting tools, a stone bead, and in the pit's lowest layer, a five-centimetre-long spear point that is clearly related to older points found to the south. By the dig's end the archaeologists knew they had uncovered the site of the oldest human habitation in British Columbia and the longest continuously occupied human site in Canada.

Of his work as an archaeologist, Driver says: "I used to think archaeology was a luxury. Now, I think it's a psychological necessity to have a past, to know it, to make connections. If you don't have a sense of the past, you're really missing something. I mean, you're standing in the bottom of the pit and above you – stacked one on top of the other – are bits of cultures that span over 10,000 years."

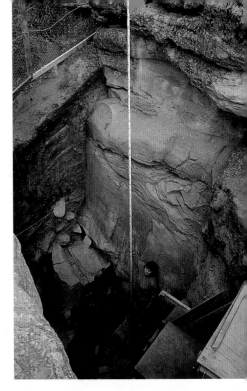

Five metres deep in British Columbia's Charlie Lake Cave excavation pit northwest of Fort St. John, an archaeologist stands near bedrock with human artifacts from past millennia above her. The site contains the debris of almost 10,500 years of continuous occupation of the small cave.
JONATHAN DRIVER

Enchantment is nature's song heard by a sensitive human ear, and it is the crafted work of human hands reflecting their admiration of nature's geometries.

– THOMAS MOORE, *THE RE-ENCHANTMENT OF EVERYDAY LIFE*

Beverley

LOON CALLS ON GWILIM LAKE, BRITISH COLUMBIA. There is no mistaking the call of the loon, echoing across the lake at dusk. It is a complex and prolonged call, haunting and lonesome, that touches more than the ear. It is a sound that links past and present, for loons are the most primitive of birds, belonging to a family that evolved 50 million years ago. Sounds, like aromas, automatically evoke memories and their connected emotions. The call of the loon this evening unlocks an archive of images from childhood summers on Loon Lake, Saskatchewan. But I wonder what other parts of me, primitive and unknown, are also stirred by this ancient sound.

Our time in the wilderness has changed my sense of hearing as my ears have recovered from the mild, unnoticed deafness that sets in after prolonged exposure to the drone of the city. The tiny hairs of the inner ear are flattened by loud noise, but in the quiet of nature they start to stand up straight again, like grass recovering after being steamrolled. The result of this is more acute hearing and the ability to distinguish layers of sound – the close lapping of the lake, the chattering of a squirrel 100 metres away, the strange laughter of the loon rippling across the water.

"Every animal has a place in the frequency spectrum," says Vancouver acoustic ecologist and composer Hildegard Westerkamp. "Animals don't usually overlap with each other. They occupy their own space. Their sounds are separated by frequency, time, or both." She told me of the work of an American colleague who recorded the cacophonous sounds of Amazon birds and insects. This research led to the "niche hypothesis," which holds that wild creatures' "sound territories" are as distinct as are their physical territories. The croaking boreal chorus frogs of Elk Island fill the evening and night with their song but, except for the occasional deep-voiced bullfrog, they stop in the morning when the birds, which occupy the same frequency, begin.

Westerkamp used to bring a tape recorder to the wilderness in the same way that other people would bring a camera. Now she brings neither. "A microphone and headphones puts something between me and the natural environment," she says. "I'd rather just take my ears now." ❖

In an evening landscape not so different from a Canadian Group of Seven painting, the only thing missing is a loon's distinctive, and somewhat tragic, call. GREIF-CZOLOWSKI PHOTOGRAPHY

The Creation
is never over.
It had a beginning
but it has no
ending. Creation
is always busy
making new
scenes, new things,
and new Worlds.

– IMMANUEL KANT, *A GENERAL NATURAL HISTORY OF THE HEAVENS*

"I have very bad news for you. Are you man enough to take it?"
"God, No!" screamed Yossarian. "I'll go right to pieces."

– JOSEPH HELLER, *CATCH-22*

Daniel

OVER THE ICEFIELD OUTSIDE DESTRUCTION BAY, YUKON. Curly-haired Andy Williams, 54, bush pilot and station manager of the Yukon's Arctic Institute, has a reputation for being droll. He describes himself as "a big fish in a very small pond." "A big fish" refers to his job ferrying glaciologists, mountaineers, and the occasional leery writers into the vast, unforgiving 31,000-square-kilometre Kluane icefields; "a very small pond" refers to Destruction Bay, population 12. After checking to make sure that we are belted in, he steps out of his aging ski-equipped Helio Courier, thumps something out of sight on the fuselage, returns, has trouble latching his door, taps the glass on some cockpit dials, leans forward, eyes the offending needle, and taps some more.

"You *have* flown this before?" I ask.

"Oh, yeah," he says. "It *always* comes back." He turns a crank above his head. "The rubber band," he adds, as though to reassure us.

The plane lifts from the gravel strip, banks over aquamarine Kluane Lake, and climbs up toward the snow-covered Front Range. Below, the bearberries and buckbrush are turning burgundy in the September air. Higher still – the altimeter reads 9,300 feet – and the tan talus slopes yield to lifeless ridges and cliffs amid scores of unnamed mountains. Williams has flown here thousands of times. He loves this land's starkness, its vastness, its existential emptiness. Except for a peculiar 1.5-centimetre-long algae-eating ice worm, *nothing* lives here. Ahead now stretches a seemingly endless snow-covered plateau punctuated by blue-black crevices and the summits of enormous mountains, 25 of them over 4,200 metres high, whose bare ridges cut like black lightning bolts through the icefield. Where the ice flows over submerged mountains, it is riven with dozens of parallel fissures that descend into a cerulean blue. In all directions – ahead 100 kilometres, to the left and right 100 kilometres – snow and ice over 1,000 metres deep.

Except for the airplane's drone there is silence. The panorama is astounding. We are flying over another planet – a cold place located, it would appear, out beyond Neptune. And in a way this

PAGE 116 The five-kilometre-wide Kaskawulsh Glacier flows out of the Yukon's St. Elias Mountains. Here is the last evidence of the Ice Age, a vast and virtually lifeless plateau of 1,000-metre-deep snow and ice. DANIEL WOOD

118   WESTERN JOURNEYS

is true: Kluane is North America's last vestige of the Ice Age, a cold reminder of a time, not long ago in geologic terms, when 13 million square kilometres of Canada, an area the size of Antarctica, was covered with glaciers. Ahead rises 5,950-metre Mount Logan, the country's highest peak.

No one knows (although theories abound) what caused the four periods of worldwide glaciation that have occurred over the past two million years. They began very suddenly and ended just as suddenly. In all likelihood, I find myself thinking, it will happen again. Today's global warming will, in time, become tomorrow's global cooling as a fifth Ice Age first descends along the valleys we have just passed, moving inexorably southward with its load of ice worms. ⊞

Eventually, all things merge into one, and a river runs through it.

– NORMAN MACLEAN, *A RIVER RUNS THROUGH IT*

Beverley

AMID WHITE WATER ON THE ALSEK RIVER NEAR HAINES JUNCTION, YUKON. Jill Pangman, 43, is singing: "Summertime, and da' livin' is easy . . . " But we know that this isn't a good sign. She had warned us earlier: "Sometimes I sing when I get . . . concerned. Helps regulate my breathing." She is hauling on the 700-kilogram Zodiac's twin oars while we lamely paddle the raft over the silt-grey waters of the Alsek River, heading southward to Lowell Lake. We are approaching the only part of our trip during which the river increases in difficulty from Class 1 to Class 3. This means serious water – two-metre-high standing waves, mid-river boulders, whirlpools. Like British Columbia's Fraser River or Alberta's Athabasca River, the Yukon's Alsek River is immensely powerful. The raft, loaded with us and all our gear, is seemingly at its mercy. Daniel starts to hum, too.

Everything on this early September day is larger-than-life, more vivid than Technicolor. The valley is three kilometres across; shocks of jasmine-yellow trembling aspen line the descending creeks; above the tree line, 2,500-metre-high mountains are streaked with mahogany and oxblood as 200 species of alpine flora change colour. Ahead lies the edge of the world's largest nonpolar icefield. Here, in part of the biggest protected area in the world – 8.5 million hectares in the Yukon, British Columbia, and Alaska – it seems the wilderness goes on forever. I feel miniscule.

These rotting bones of beached
icebergs line the shoreline of
Kluane National Park's frigid
Lowell Lake. The bergs originally
calved off the adjacent 90-metre-
high face of Lowell Glacier
which, at 70 kilometres, is the
world's longest nonpolar glacier.
RON WATTS/FIRST LIGHT

The Alsek, which winds through the Yukon and British Columbia before spilling into the Pacific Ocean at Dry Bay, Alaska, 270 kilometres from its source, is carrying us through a land that encompasses nature's extremes: as much as 19 hours of daylight and plus 33 degrees Celsius in the summer, as little as four hours of daylight and minus 50 degrees Celsius in the winter. There are frequent floods, rainstorms, avalanches, and landslides here. The species that thrive in this place, including homo sapiens, are a breed apart. "I love the wildness of it," Pangman says as she warns us of the pontoon-piercing boulders around the next bend. The wind, so strong yesterday that we didn't launch the raft, is again blowing toward us. My shoulders ache. We have been paddling for eight hours and still have one more to go. I watch Pangman, straining against the wind and the white water, and remember what she had told me when I had asked about fear and fatigue. "I breathe the power of the river," she had said. "I breathe it in so I can work with it rather than being overpowered." I keep paddling. Keep breathing. The Zodiac pitches. Boulders and standing waves appear . . . dead ahead. Pangman shouts orders: "Back-paddle! Back-paddle!" It is hard to hear her above the river's roar. She stands to survey the line through the grey turmoil.

Finally we reach Lowell Lake, a blue-and-white world of sculpted icebergs – the enormous icy calves of Lowell Glacier, which curves along a five-kilometre perimeter of the lake to our right. Some of the icebergs are the size of stadiums, others the size of cars. The lake is filled with them. A big one keels over with a thunderous splash, revealing a different shape and a new play of shadow on ice. Others, backlit by the sun setting behind the St. Elias Mountains, are either as translucent as fine porcelain or marbled with streaks of pink and celadon.

That night around the campfire Pangman describes seeing one-quarter of the sky filled with swirling colour; this occurred near Old Crow, 750 kilometres north of here. For an hour, she said, there had been curtains of shimmering pinks and greens and electric-white vortices. We make a pact that anyone getting up in the night and seeing the aurora borealis will wake the others.

In my tent, on the edge of sleep, I can see Pangman silhouetted against the flames, alone. I drift off to the sound of her playing "Amazing Grace" on her harmonica. I awake on occasion to the crash of nearby icebergs toppling over and peer outside into the cold and dark, but there are only stars. The next morning I learn that we were, indeed, visited during the night: not by aurora borealis but by *Ursus arctos horribilis*. ❧

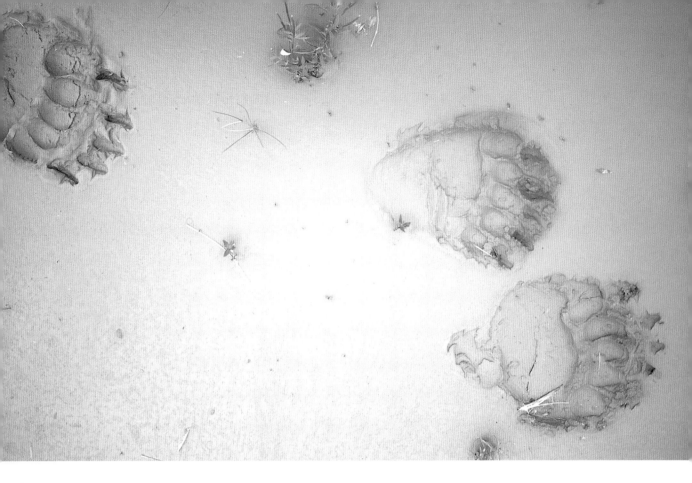

Want to know the best way to stop a grizzly?
When he gets REAL *close, you reach down his*
throat an' grab his asshole an' pull him inside out.

– ART PAPINEAU, YUKON GOLD MINER

Daniel

GRIZZLY TRACKS AT LOWELL LAKE IN THE YUKON'S KLUANE NATIONAL PARK. The signs of grizzlies are everywhere. A week ago a set of tracks emerged from the nearby Tatshenshini River, circled the spot where the bear had eaten a salmon, and disappeared into the spruce forest. Our guide that day, 53-year-old Southern Tutchone Native Chuck Hume, said he could smell the bear; it was that close. He added that several years earlier a grizzly had charged from the same copse of trees and had shoulder-checked him so hard that he had flown 10 metres through the air. A couple of days later, pitching our tent, we'd noticed another set of fresh prints 30 metres away amid the willows along the Dezadeash River. Yesterday there were a half-dozen fresh sets crossing the muddy pans below 1,680-metre-high Goatherd Mountain (where we had camped). Some of the larger tracks, I had noted with amusement, were three times as large as my outstretched hand.

"Pretty big," Beverley had said, her voice's inflection rising ominously.

These 20-centimetre-long reminders of a nocturnal tentside visitor to the shore of Lowell Lake evoke the old, atavistic fears that once propelled Neolithic humans into caves. The reality is: bear attacks, by grizzlies or blacks, are very, very rare.
DANIEL WOOD

I told her that she had a way with words, then I stood and surveyed the desolate moraine-scape around us, looking for movement . . . large, furry, four-legged movement. I know grizzlies can run at bursts of up to 50 kilometres per hour. Every distant bear-size boulder seemed to quiver. But none moved.

And now, camped at the southern end of Lowell Lake with scores of enormous icebergs beached just offshore, morning brings this curious revelation: there are grizzly bear prints *atop* our Vibram-soled prints. I know that, although there are over 200 grizzlies in Kluane, attacks against humans are very rare. I also know, having tracked wolves in Alberta and cougars on Vancouver Island, that one can dismiss danger too easily. Since then, a pack of wolves has killed an Ontario naturalist and a cougar a B.C. woman. So the grizzly tracks concentrate the mind and dredge up the old atavisms, the old vulnerabilities. The footprints are almost humanoid, since the bear shares with humankind a rare mammalian trait: walking plantigrade – heel, ball of foot, nubbly toes. Here, the tracks inform us, a cub follows its mother. Over there, a big male leaves 10-centimetre-deep craters in the mud. It is easy, here in the Yukon wilderness, to imagine how Neolithic people felt in the presence of such tracks and why stories of the Sasquatch still survive in the continent's Northwest. The deep tracks of dangerous predators contain numinous shadows and, if one looks closely, claws. ⊞

Few natural phenomena have inspired more myths than the aurora. Seen by some as omens, by others as sky-borne animal spirits, and still others as celestial torches guiding the newly dead toward afterlife, the aurora borealis writes stories in the night sky. TESSA MACINTOSH/NWT GOVERNMENT

NIGHT LIGHTS

Often I just hurt from the awe and beauty and wondrous mystery of the lights . . .

– ROBERT EATHER, *MAJESTIC LIGHTS*

A small sampling of what the world's myths and legends have to say about the northern lights: they are the dancing spirits of beluga whales; the souls of those who have died from loss of blood, for example, in childbirth; the light of angels; torches used by spirits to spear fish at night; warnings of God's wrath; light captured by glaciers during the long summer days and released in the dark of winter; the souls of the dead beckoning new arrivals; the breath of warriors battling in the sky; or the long-dead playing soccer, using a human or walrus skull for a ball. They are said to cause heart attacks; to increase psychiatric disturbances; to snatch your children away when you are not looking; to increase extrasensory perception; and to warn of illness, death, plague, war, and/or the presence of fairies. To see the shimmering colours of the aurora borealis sweeping across the sky is to see what Robert Service describes as "a sight for the eyes of God."

It is also to see a phenomenon that has puzzled scientists since Galileo Galilei sky-gazed more than 400 years ago. Today the northern lights are known to be caused by solar wind – a spray of magnetically-charged particles from the sun that rushes through space at three million kilometres per hour

before colliding with Earth's upper atmosphere. Spinning downward along invisible magnetic polar force fields, these high-speed electrons strike high-altitude oxygen and nitrogen atoms 400 to 1,000 kilometres above the Earth. These, in turn, acquire an electrifying (and visible) charge. The agitated atmospheric atoms strike adjacent atoms like quintillions of mad bumper cars. Each atom momentarily lights up. Currents of light, like eddies in a rushing river, flow across the sky.

Swirls . . . curtains . . . pinwheels . . . streaks . . . ribbons of colour: green, white, yellow, and (sometimes) red. Depending on conditions, the lower edge of the visible light is 90 to 150 kilometres above the ground.

This is happening all the time, 24 hours a day, every day, producing auroral ovals around both the North and South Poles. Those who live close to the poles have a much greater likelihood of seeing the northern lights than do those who do not. For example, if it were not for

clouds and the midnight sun, people living in Alberta's extreme north would be able to see the lights 300 nights per year, while those living in southern Alberta are very lucky to see them 30 nights per year. The lights tend to be slightly more visible around the spring and fall equinoxes, with particularly vivid auroras coming at 27-day intervals. The northern lights' 11-year cycle matches that of sunspot activity; the last peak occurred in 1991.

Civilization exists by geological consent, subject to change without notice.

– WILL DURANT, HISTORIAN

Daniel

THE SURGING GLACIER, LOWELL LAKE, YUKON. As the helicopter lifts upward, the story of the cataclysm unfolds like a pop-up picture book. To the right is 1,700-metre-high Goatherd Mountain. To the left is 70-kilometre-long Lowell Glacier. In between and below is Lowell Lake, studded with icebergs. Around the year 1725 the massive river of ice to my left, the world's longest nonpolar glacier, began moving. Most likely buoyed up on a lubricating veneer of sub-glacial water, the 4.5-kilometre-wide, 100-metre-high icefield surged across the intervening lake and collided with the vertical face of Goatherd Mountain, damming the Alsek River. (Studies have revealed four previous surges.) Over the following 125 years, the river formed a 75-kilometre-long lake, known to glaciologists as Recent Lake Alsek – No. 5. The lake was a natural disaster waiting to happen. Around the year 1850 the ice dam broke. In less than 48 hours 260 cubic kilometres of water raced down the Alsek Valley, producing a number of unusual phenomena.

I count at least 19 different gravelly benches below, each distinguished by curious horizontal and parallel lines of fireweed, sage, and aspen. The mountainsides look as though they had been planted by a misguided farmer. These benches mark the lake's old beaches, now 30, 40, 50 metres above today's meandering Alsek River. In places the slopes below are littered with blackening driftwood logs, as though Noah had landed here. And huge blocks of white marble, rafted onto the vanished lake atop icebergs that calved from the Lowell Glacier, record the spots where the bergs once melted. Tree-ring counting shows that none of the yellowing aspen along the river's banks are more than 150 years old.

Most strange of all are the runaway river's ripple marks. Where currents of moving water hit sand or gravel, small ripples are naturally produced, typically five to six centimetres high. The ripples below the helicopter, however, are five to six *metres* high, a testament to the forces unleashed here. The torrent obliterated Native villages, killing scores before reaching the Gulf of Alaska 270 kilometres away. Early ethnologists, modern research has revealed, were mystified by 19th-century Native accounts of this flood.

The view downward on this calm September day reveals the simple patterns inscribed on the land. Enormous fans of lichen-covered talus spread outward from the unnamed 2,500-metre-high mountains that surround us. Every slope of talus and skree has assumed an almost identical angle: 35 degrees from the horizontal. Called, in geological terms, the angle of repose, it records the planet-wide restraint that friction imposes on gravity, the sloping line where falling things come to rest. Below these, the deltas of descending creeks meet the braided shallow water of the Alsek River, free again to meander. The river's channels are silver-blue, like the veins visible in my wrist. The subtext of height is pattern – the virtue and the comfort of the long view. 🔲

FOLLOWING PAGES In the first weeks of September the Yukon goes through a metamorphosis: the bearberries go burgundy, the aspens and willows yellow, as the North's brief summer explodes in a final pyrotechnical display of brilliant colours. RICHARD HART-MIER/FIRST LIGHT

A translucent three-story-high iceberg drifts amid hundreds of others on Kluane National Park's remote Lowell Lake. Seldom an hour passes here without the booming cannonade of the nearby Lowell Glacier calving or one of the icebergs turning turtle amid a loud, watery explosion. DANIEL WOOD

A CATACLYSM INSCRIBED IN ICE

One of the strangest phenomena in the West, and a natural feature unique on Earth, is the slow-moving forest of white spruce, willow, and poplar that grows atop the Klutlan Glacier in the Yukon's Kluane Wildlife Sanctuary. The forest of 10-metre-high trees, and its attendant population of animals and birds, owes its precarious existence to a volcanic eruption 10 times bigger than the 1980 Mount St. Helens blast. Vulca-

nologists say that around 770 A.D. Alaska's Mount Churchill exploded, covering much of northwestern Canada with a layer of pumice known as the White River Ash. The debris piled up a half-metre deep on the nearby Klutlan Glacier and, in time, seeds took hold and grew into a 25-square-kilometre forest, complete with the only known examples of moose, caribou, wolves, and birds that live on top of ice. Standing at the five-kilometre-long toe of the glacier – the widest continental

ice front outside the arctic regions – the eye, scanning upward, reads the story. First, a vertical wall of crevice-filled blue-grey ice laced the descending, exposed roots of trees. Then came a layer of grey ash and darker dirt above. Finally, high above, stands the boreal forest at the glacier's edge, destined to plunge downward as the ice retreats.

WINTER ADAPTATION OF PLANTS

When does winter start around here? Any minute now.

– ANDY WILLIAMS, BUSH PILOT

"Everything that lives here has to adapt to the weather," says Bruce Bennett, a plant-community technician with the Canadian Wildlife Service in Whitehorse. "It's going to grow low, grow fast, follow the sun, be fuzzy, cut out UV rays – some or all of those things." In fact, the plants of the North make all others look wimpy. The common trees of the Yukon – lodgepole pine, trembling aspen, black and white spruce, birch, tamarack, balsam poplar – can withstand temperatures as low as minus 80 degrees Celsius. A Douglas fir on the southwest B.C. coast begins to die if the temperature drops much lower than about minus 20 degrees Celsius. The shorter and colder days of fall trigger changes in the metabolism of the northern trees, including an increase in the plant hormone ABA, a photoactive hormone that increases dramatically as day length decreases and water becomes less available. This hormone does a couple of things that are crucial to acclimation: it inhibits growth and it increases the permeability of membranes to water, which helps to prevent intracellular ice formation.

The Yukon's prairie crocus has a fuzzy coating on its leaves and stems and is heliotropic, which means that the warming rays of the sun are directed into the centre of the flower. Ants and beetles crawl into the bloom to keep warm at the end of April; in the process of squiggling around and getting comfortable, the insects pick up pollen, which they subsequently transplant to other flowers. When the plant is about 60 centimetres tall, it produces a fluffy seed head known as a "towhead baby." The seed head collects heat so effectively that it is 10 degrees Celsius warmer inside than outside the plant.

Tricuspid saxifrage, which looks like a mat of fuzzy leaves, is common in dry arctic areas and grows low to the ground, as do many tundra plants, in order to reduce desiccation from wind. Surviving in the most barren of soils, it also has a built-in composting system: the leaves grow tightly together so that the ones that die stay on the plant and provide it with nutrients.

The leaves and needles of many northern trees – subalpine fir, white spruce, and some willows – have a bluish tinge indicative of the plant world's version of sunblock. "Bloom," as it is called, is a waxy coating secreted by the cuticle, and it helps cut down on the ultraviolet radiation that could damage growing tissue in the summer months when the sun shines for up to 24 hours a day. This is also the reason that the needles on arctic subalpine fir are vertical rather than horizontal (as are those of fir trees farther south).

Richardson's pond weed, common in the lakes around Old Crow in the Yukon's north, takes advantage of every second of the 24-hour summer sunlight. It has a growing season of just one month. The plant is killed by the cold, but its buried rhizomes lie dormant until the water temperature warms up. Then a storehouse of energy is unleashed and the pond weed grows up to 30 centimetres a day.

Daniel

FLYING INSIDE THE STIKINE CANYON NEAR TELE-GRAPH CREEK, BRITISH COLUMBIA. There are, I know, many ways to die. But at the moment it appears I may go doing a high-speed face-plant against a sheer 300-metre-high cliff. In my headphones I hear pilot Casey Buckles hollering, "Let's rock 'n' roll." The helicopter suddenly banks, its skids seeming to brush the vertical rock. I get a sideward glimpse of light ahead, a slot with the grey-brown Stikine River boiling directly below and a strand of lapis lazuli sky above. The helicopter levels out and I am treated to the view of an impossibly narrow canyon – dead ahead. "Let's rock 'n' roll!" Buckles shouts. I have just enough time to think that I am the captive of an airborne madman before we plunge into the cleft, like Luke Skywalker in *Star Wars*. Yes, God, *please,* may the Force be with me, I think. I hear myself whooping between exhilaration and terror, and I hear Buckles's voice in my headphones, laughing at me and at the g-forces that press us into our seats.

Only a few people have seen the inside of the remote 96-kilometre-long Stikine gorge, known as the Grand Canyon of Canada. Its inaccessibility prevents exploration. This section of the Stikine, one of the continent's last great untamed rivers, is a place of vertiginous grey-black basalt precipices, whirlpools, standing waves, and awesome rapids. Only a few kayaks have navigated this maelstrom. No salmon migrate through the canyon. No roads approach the chasm. Unlike the impressive canyon of the Tatshenshini River, which rafters regularly run, and the Fraser Canyon, seen by millions of motorists, the Stikine's canyon is a dark, deep aperture in the earth, seen mostly by eagles or cliff-dwelling mountain goats. ⊞

WHEN THE ICE EXPLODES

As the inhabitants of the North know, there comes a day, usually in May, when the river ice breaks up. The event is often dramatic and sometimes destructive. The spring meltwater, rising beneath two or three metres of winter ice, forces the frozen surface upward. When it finally ruptures in thunderous cannonades and end-of-the-world shrieking, the jagged blocks of ice begin their downstream journey. They bang against each other. They squeak and groan. At times, the ice jams up and the river overflows its banks. Usually, however, over the course of an hour or a day, the noisy parade passes. The departure of the ice is an annual reassurance that winter, even in the True North, doesn't last forever.

The migration of caribou across the Yukon's tundra – like the migration of scores of other animals, from butterflies to whales – demonstrates that many wild creatures have a variety of sensory skills unknown to humans. TIM FITZHARRIS/MASTERFILE

FOLLOWING INVISIBLE CLUES: SEEING THE FUTURE THROUGH INSTINCT

The movement of animals – mammals, fish, birds, insects – across enormous distances is the stuff of mystery and wonder. Somehow it happens: a salmon returns to the exact creek where it was born; a caribou crosses a snowmelt-swollen Yukon river at precisely the same spot year after year. Humankind, insulated from seasonal rhythms and nature's discrete messages (consisting of such phenomena as magnetism, chemical odours, infrared light, and slight shifts in temperature), is left to speculate on the sensory clues that wild creatures use to migrate over thousands of unsignposted kilometres. Modern research has revealed that insects and fish can "read" polarized light; that birds observe star patterns; that snakes "see" infrared heat; that sturgeon can navigate using electro-receptors sensitive to miniscule electrical charges; that slugs, sharks, and birds utilize magnetism to determine direction; and that salmon fingerlings imprint on the chemical "smell" of their home stream. Of the numerous examples of animal migration in the West, here are a few out-standing cases:

▸ Over 100,000 Porcupine Herd caribou head southward from

It was like the first morning when God saw that it was good.

– MALCOLM LOWRY, *UNDER THE VOLCANO*

Daniel

CLIMBING MOUNT EDZIZA'S EVE CONE OUTSIDE ISKUT, BRITISH COLUMBIA. We have come in low and we have come in fast; the gauge in front of me reads 130 miles per hour. The hummocky flows of hardened lava, visible at a higher altitude as distinct sinuous black rivers snaking down toward us from 2,787-metre-high Mount Edziza, the massive shield volcano of British Columbia's northwest, are now blurred by speed and proximity. If there were trees on this tundralike terrain, then the helicopter's rotor would be clearcutting them. Ahead, rising up in front of us like a miniature Mount Fuji, is Eve Cone, a perfectly symmetrical inverted funnel of jet-black pumice.

The pilot, bearded 54-year-old Manley Fredlund, spirals us up and over the volcano's lip, then down inside its lifeless crater. The turn is tight, the horizon wonky. I look down into a cauldera the colour of old bricks: rust going grey. I try to imagine the

the Alaska-Yukon arctic tundra each autumn into the warmer spruce of the subarctic boreal forest. Over the millennia their footsteps have worn visible pathways in the solid rock. With the herds of plains bison decimated, the annual movement of caribou across the central Yukon is the last great land mammal migration on the continent.

▸ Between mid-March and late April an estimated 20,000 grey whales pass the B.C. coast on their 10,000-kilometre journey from the Baja California calving grounds to the nutrient-rich Bering Sea.

▸ Every decade or so painted lady butterflies migrate northward

from the United States into Alberta, arriving in springtime flocks of millions. They disperse across the province, covering the land in vibrant black, white, and orange-red wings.

▸ The natural north-south corridors that cross the region are aerial avenues for millions of migrating birds that utilize coastal estuaries and inland marshes for refuelling stops on their annual journeys over thousands of kilometres. Many migratory birds, like the whooping crane, are known to return to the exact same nesting sites throughout their lives.

FOLLOWING PAGES Only the thinnest veneer of grass and tiny clumps of moss campion grow around remote Eve Cone where, 1,300 years ago, huge rivers of lava flowed and pumice buried the slopes of nearby Mount Edziza. GARY FIEGEHEN

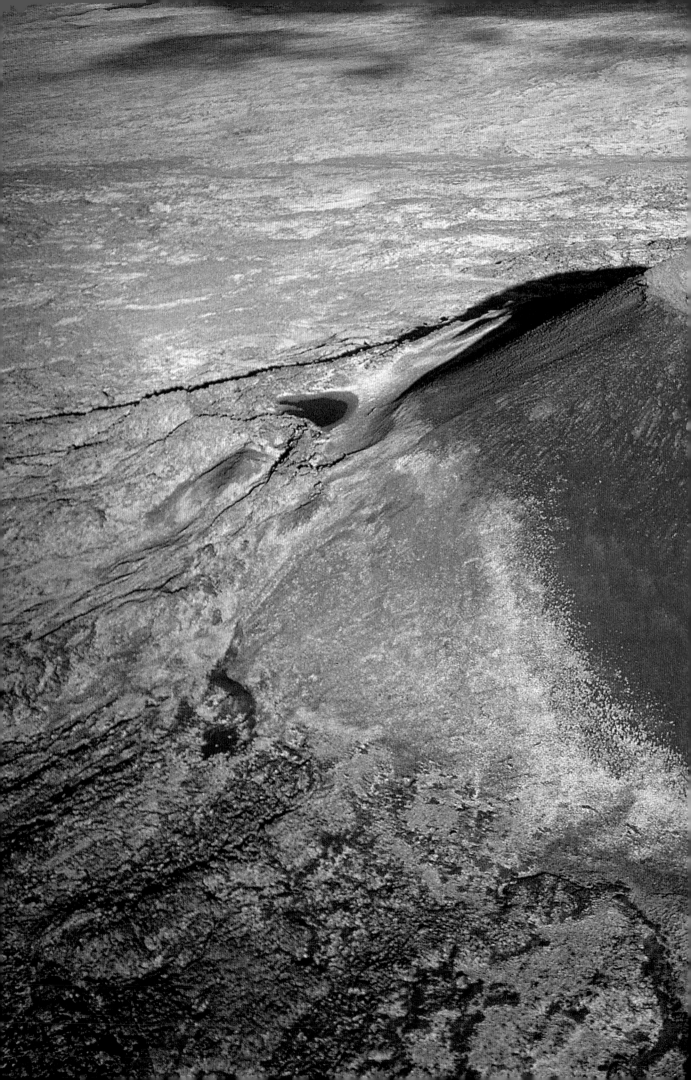

scene here 1,300 years ago when this cone, and the adjacent and suitably named Chocolate and Coffee Cones, were erupting and incandescent rivers of lava were meandering downhill.

On the ground, the helicopter silenced, the igneous moonscape is bleak: blocks of black pumice and black pyroclastic bombs, black lava flows, black sand, and the thinnest veneer of yellowing grasses (reminiscent of a sheet thrown over a corpse). Above me, 150-metre-high Eve Cone rises abruptly, its geometry formed by twin parabolas and its mass filling half the overcast sky. I begin climbing. Within a few steps I discover several things about ascending a volcano. One: it is steep. The loose pumice's angle of repose, 35 degrees from the horizontal, is not the angle of repose for the human heart. Two: the loose cobbles are sharp, and climbing the slope is like climbing a hill of unconsolidated broken bottles. Every step produces a small avalanche of debris from higher up; every stumble produces a new scrape. Three: pride, especially stupid male pride, has its price. Propelled now by the eyes watching my seemingly inebriated ascent from below and my own dogged, testosterone-ravaged ambition, I reach the volcano's lip only to find, balancing there, the even-steeper-sided cliff of the caldera. *Whoooa!*

Fredlund takes this opportunity to join me at ringside – in his helicopter. I watch the aerial acrobatics and feel the rotor wash as he sweeps up, over, around, circling, lifting, banking, hovering above little, semifrightened me and the little, exquisite volcano. I recall what he had said to me earlier about his love of helicopter flying and comfort myself that things will turn out all right now: "The air is full of unlimited pathways. You make your own path. You live in three-dimension. You're on the edge. And in control."

We exchange waves, a couple of middle-aged men delighted to be in three dimensions: on our own path; on the edge; and, except for a few minor cuts to my palms, in control. ⊞

VII ON THE PERIMETER OF THE DEEP:

QUEEN CHARLOTTE ISLANDS AND THE NORTHWESTERN B.C. COAST

We shall not cease
from exploration
And the end of all
our exploring
Will be to arrive
where we started
And know the place
for the first time.

– T. S. ELIOT, *FOUR QUARTETS*

The next disaster will occur at about the time the last one has been forgotten.

– ANCIENT JAPANESE PROVERB

ABOVE The spectral image of a Native spirit decorates an old totem pole outside Hazelton. The nearby Nisga'a Memorial Lava Bed, the result of Canada's most recent volcanic eruption, marks the site where 2,000 Nisga'a died just 300 years ago. DANIEL WOOD

PAGE 138 The 25-centimetre-wide aggregating anemone congregates on rock walls and boulders near the low-tide line. Reproducing asexually, the ensuing identical offspring usually cluster around the "parent." If an individual from another, unrelated anemone comes near, there will be a fight.

JASON PUDDIFOOT/FIRST LIGHT

WITH THE DEAD AT THE NISGA'A MEMORIAL LAVA BED, NORTH OF TERRACE, BRITISH COLUMBIA. Everyone here knows the myth. The volcanic eruption was Canada's most recent and most disastrous. It happened only 300 years ago, maybe less, not long before European contact – recent history, as time is measured in terms of both geological change and myth. The story says that children were jabbing burning hemlock twigs into the salmon migrating up the nearby Tseax River and laughing as the fish swam toward their spawning grounds with flames on their backs. The Nisga'a chief warned them not to break their respectful relationship with nature. "Something will befall us," he'd said. The children, however, continued their play. Soon the ground began to rumble and white-hot, 1,200-degree-Celsius lava from what is now called Wil Ksi Ba<u>x</u>hl Mihl (Where the Fire Ran Out) spilled westward for 20 kilometres down the Tseax River, effectively damming it. There it met the larger Nass River and stopped, forming a 10-metre-high lava cliff. The now-solid lava flow upon which we walk – 35 metres thick in some places, 11 kilometres long, and five kilometres wide – left 2,000 Native people dead.

Here, surrounded by the lush Nass Valley, the land is barren and surreal, consisting of almost 18,000 hectares of craters, cinder cones, small turquoise or ash-grey pools, crevasses, and caves. A moonscape with a little moss, cactuslike stonecrop, and a few ferns; small pines, cedars, and cottonwoods struggle between the rocks. Lichen covers clumps and boulders of lava like a thick blanket of ash. Erosion and vegetation haven't had time to soften the edges of the igneous rock, so five-metre-long tree moulds – perfect casts of the trees that once grew here – remain, marking the site of the incinerated forest. As we walk upon sheets of relatively smooth rock, the "skin" of lava that cooled above the liquid core, our footsteps sound hollow, as though we are crossing a drum. Two eagles circle overhead and one grasshopper jumps away – other than the vegetation, the only signs of life. Everywhere huge slabs of lava are piled against one another like fallen tombstones. ❧

FUNGI 'R' US

British Columbia, with its wide range of topography and temperate climate, is one of the world's great regions for mycologists. Over 10,000 different types of fungi grow in the province. According to 42-year-old mushroom expert Paul Kroeger, whose lifelong interest in mushrooms was sparked by their serendipitous nature – "They pop up so unpredictably," he says – the same precipitation that supports gigantic rainforest trees supports gigantic fungi and mushrooms. Kroeger has encountered bracket fungus about a metre across on the trunk of a dying conifer as well as a 40-centimetre-wide Boletus mushroom, looking like an oversize brown Frisbee, in Vancouver's Stanley Park. And he recalls seeing, in a Wetaskiwin, Alberta, museum, a faded, circa 1920s photograph of a 1.5-metre-wide giant puffball mushroom sitting atop the roof of a Model T.

Four distinct colours of lichen and algae – white, orange, grey, and green – illustrate the fecundity of the British Columbia coast. Unlike most plants that live from the soil, lichen cultivate algae that provide the primitive plant with nutrients.
AL HARVEY

Those who follow the natural order flow in the current of Tao.

– HUAI NAN TZU

Beverley

WITH THE SPAWNING SALMON NEAR KITIMAT, BRITISH COLUMBIA. I am still curled inside my sleeping bag when Norm Wagner, 34, asks if I want sweetener in my coffee. I say no. He says, "Not even Bailey's?" and I know, despite the rain, that this is going to be a good day. He has just adjusted the automatic pilot of the *Exodus,* a 10-metre trimaran, to enable us to start our southward journey.

The air is grey, the water is grey, the sky is grey, the clouds are grey, the rocks are grey, the seals are grey – all of which provides a strangely soothing balm for eyes used to the sensory overload of urban landscapes. The monochromatic surroundings gradually induce a feeling of calm, perhaps assisted by a little more Bailey's and the dreamlike sensation of floating on the mirror-flat waters of the Douglas Channel. Time passes. Or maybe it stands still and the land passes. We finally drop anchor at the mouth of an unnamed creek and lower the dinghy to take us upstream.

Above us, Wagner assures me, snowcapped 2,000-metre-high mountains are hidden under the shroud of fog. The rainforest surrounds us. The trees are spectral. We pull the boat up onto a gravel bar. "Looks like somebody thinks this is a good

PREVIOUS PAGES These two spawning Adams River sockeye salmon will soon die. But their offspring will return, after thousands of kilometres of travel and the passage of years, to the precise gravelly riverbed where they were born. GRAHAM OSBORNE

BELOW A solitary hiker on the Queen Charlotte Islands' desolate Naikoon (or East) Beach encounters one shipwreck and nine creeks on his way to Rose Spit, 94 kilometres and six days north of the trailhead at Tlell. GREIF-CZOLOWSKI PHOTOGRAPHY

fishing hole," he says. A few metres away a seagull plucks the eyes out of a still-flopping salmon caught just moments ago by one of the black bears whose prints are everywhere on the beach.

We continue upriver, and suddenly they are there below us. First just a few, then so many pink and chum salmon that I can barely see the cobbles on the creek bottom. They swim under the boat and on all sides, first one, then five more, then 10, then 100, then too many to count. I think, crazily, that I could walk to shore on their backs or, like a bear, plunge my arm into the water and haul a few out. They are fighting their way upstream away from the Pacific, pausing here, darting a little farther there, aiming for the safety of a deep pool, resting briefly, then fighting again through rapids, swimming hard for a few metres, pausing, swimming again, not stopping to feed, moving (on average) 22 hours a day. Instinct and the identifiable smell of their home stream pulls them to spawn here in the water they left two or three years ago and in which they will soon die. They are so close that their every detail is visible: the fixed eyes, the skin ripped by rocks. And, in keeping with today's palette, these salmon aren't the bright crimson of spawning sockeye but a muted greenish-grey – a phalanx of underwater shadows. ❈

WILDERNESS WALKING ON ENDLESS NAIKOON BEACH

I grow old . . . I grow old . . .
I shall wear the bottoms of my
*   trousers rolled. . . .*
I shall wear white flannel
*   trousers, and walk upon the*
*   beach.*
I have heard the mermaids
*   singing, each to each.*

    – T. S. ELIOT, "THE LOVE SONG
    OF J. ALFRED PRUFROCK"

If British Columbia's coastline were straightened out, it would measure 27,200 kilometres – two-thirds the distance of the Earth's equator. As mariners and landlubbers alike know, most of this shoreline is kelp-lined, barnacle-scabbed rock.

Beaches are rare. Especially the kind of sandy beaches long enough and deserted enough to enable the thought-filled itinerant to walk out of himself and into spindrift's timelessness.

There are, of course, a number of lengthy well-known beach walks: Vancouver Island's Long Beach and Rathtrevor Beach and the arching, driftwood-backed spits of land on the northern end of several islands in the Strait of Georgia. None, however, compares in length or assurance of solitude to remote 94-kilometre-long Naikoon Beach (or East Beach, as it is also known) on the northeast flank of the Queen Charlotte Islands. It is one of the world's

longest wilderness beach walks, a place to spend days without encountering a soul. Its windswept desolation is its attraction, introspection its reward. The route is crossed by several bog-brown fordable rivers and is lined by driftwood, low dunes, and moss-draped cedars. Whales cruise offshore. It is six days from Tlell in the south to Rose Spit in the north and, in that time, the only sounds that intrude may be the wind in the cedars, the seagulls keening, and the sluicing of waves along Hecate Strait.

We stand on an islet in the midst of an illimitable ocean of inexplicability.

– THOMAS HUXLEY

WANDERING AMONG THE TOTEM POLES AT NINSTINTS, BRITISH COLUMBIA. Of the building once named People Think of This House Even When They Sleep Because the Master Feeds Everyone Who Calls, only the remains of the four corner posts survive. The house's totem pole has pitched forward toward the sea. Grass grows up around the carved eyes. Next door, the house once called Thunder Rolls upon It is nothing more than a two-metre-deep rectangular hole. A huge spruce has grown from the centre of one of the building's cedar corner posts, engulfing the carved wood so that tree and post are one. When Wanagun, the Haida standing beside me, first came to this place in 1973, he pulled his newly purchased Simpsons-Sears canoe onto the beach after a three-week-long paddle south. He was, he tells me, searching for himself. The place was overgrown with salmonberries and spruce. But half-concealed in the rainforest stood 25 ancient totem poles – their cedar silver with age, their carved faces the faces of Haida mythology, their sightless eyes fixed on the sea. Wanagun had built a small fire and made an offering of tobacco to the long dead. Wanagun knew the spirits were near; he knew he had come home. He says to me, with dark eyes and great conviction: "The spirits . . . they're around. If you're very quiet, if you listen . . . you will feel them."

As I walk through the old village, now listed as a UNESCO World Heritage Site because it contains the largest collection of original standing totem poles on Earth, I try to absorb the place's spirituality. Fog wreaths the spruce. Miniature deer wander unafraid. In 1790 over 300 people lived here; a century later, decimated by smallpox, the settlement was abandoned. I stand beneath a five-metre-high mortuary pole and look up. Incised into the cedar, a mythical sea grizzly holds a seal in its mouth. In a slot at the top of the pole rests a small weathered casket. One side has fallen off, revealing the box's emptiness. A salmonberry bush with emerald leaves grows from the place where once, over 150 years ago, the bones of a Haida hero were interred.

Like cultures, like some humans, cedar rots from the inside. Some of the old poles lean at precarious angles, ready to fall. I ask Wanagun whether there is any plan to save them. "No," he tells me. "All things pass. That's the way of nature." And with that he gives me a diffident shrug. ⊞

PREVIOUS PAGES The surviving totem poles at Ninstints line a forested bay now inhabited by Haida ghosts. All that is left of the 19th-century Native settlement here are moss-filled house pits and leaning mortuary poles. DANIEL WOOD

COLOURS

‣ IN THE CLEAR HILLS *of northern Alberta run iron springs the colour of fresh blood.*

‣ THE COLOURS OF BAT STARS, *common in intertidal Burnaby Narrows on the Queen Charlotte Islands, range through fuchsia, opal, lapis lazuli, iridescent twilight blue, garnet, and mottled greenish-brown.*

‣ EMERALD LAKE NEAR WHITEHORSE, *Yukon, like many other glacial lakes whose water is filled with suspended particles of glacial silt, glows an unreal turquoise.*

‣ THE ELECTRIC-PINK *of tiny moss campion flowers amid bleak high-altitude tundra is a vivid reminder of nature's tenaciousness against long odds.*

‣ THE CURLING HALF-PEELED BARK *of British Columbia's Gulf Island arbutus juxtaposes satiny lime-green wood with tissue-thin, salmon-coloured bark.*

‣ WHEN THE NEEDLES *of the mountain larch turn jasmine each September around southern British Columbia's aquamarine Cathedral Lakes, it looks like the lakeshore trees are literally on fire.*

‣ OF ALL THE MULTICOLOURED BIRDS, *the extraordinary rufous hummingbird, a rocket of iridescent orange-red, is most like ball lightning on wings.*

‣ SPRINGTIME IS ANNOUNCED *in western marshlands by the absurdly bright yellow spike of the skunk cabbage, its shaft a startling contrast to the black soil.*

‣ THE FOLDED AND MULTICOLOURED *banded metamorphic rocks in the northern flank of the Yukon's Goatherd Mountain may have no equal in the West.*

‣ THE SHOCKING SCARLET *of the autumn-blooming* Amanita muscaria *mushroom blazes like a stoplight in western woodlands.*

FOLLOWING PAGES Under the bright sun the pale sage-green of the broad-leaved stonecrop turns the vivid colour of cinnamon hearts. GRAHAM OSBORNE

At the darkest moment comes the light.

– JOSEPH CAMPBELL

Daniel

THE ABANDONED WHALING STATION AT ROSE HARBOUR, BRITISH COLUMBIA. The dog-eared annual logbook that Bronx-born Susan Wier hands me is a sobering reminder of the ghosts that inhabit the grey rain-shrouded coast of the Queen Charlotte Islands. The Native villages are mostly ruins, their populations decimated by smallpox in the 1860s and 1870s. (The 10,000 Haida of the late 1700s were reduced to 585 a century later.) The scattered utopian experiments of early white settlers are dead, too, usually destroyed by internal strife. And the logbook of Rose Harbour's Consolidated Whaling Station, covering most of the 20th century, offers a year by year account of the tens of thousands of whales that were processed here.

As my eyes scan the pages, some illustrated with yellowing photos of whales being flensed (butchered) on the nearby beach, I succumb to a visceral sadness. Great slabs of blubber unfurl from the creatures' sides as Lilliputian men swarm about the carcasses. The caption reports that a 30-metre blue whale, the largest animal ever to live on Earth, produces about 130 barrels of oil. The pages are a precise accounting of the annual harvest: blues, humpbacks, greys listed down one column; the totals of barrels of rendered oil down the other. It didn't seem to matter that, as the decades passed, the numbers in both columns decreased until, in 1967, the whaling station finally closed. The whales were virtually gone. All that remains here is a rusting five-metre-high cauldron that sits on the beach – the steam-making boiler through which the behemoths' flesh became fuel. ⊞

This rusting remnant of the abandoned Consolidated Whaling Station marks the Queen Charlotte Islands site where, for decades, whale blubber was reduced to whale oil. DANIEL WOOD

Then God spake unto the fish; and from the shuddering cold and blackness of the sea, the whale came breaching up toward the warm and pleasant sun, and all the delights of air and earth . . .

– HERMAN MELVILLE, *MOBY DICK*

Beverley

WITH THE HUMPBACK WHALES, ICEBERG BAY, BRITISH COLUMBIA. In spring, when the oolichan are running, Ken Bejcar, 39, manager of a north-coast lodge, takes his 10-metre Boston Whaler into the bay, taps the side of the boat, and is instantly surrounded by as many as 30 porpoises. This ocean wilderness, 120 kilometres from Prince Rupert and accessible only by floatplane or boat, is teeming with creatures that have gathered to feed on the oolichan. "I could be under a million seagulls," Bejcar says. "When I go by in the boat, it's like the whole beach starts to fly." Thousands of eagles, too – 15 or 20 in every tree. Twice he has seen a pod of six or eight killer whales from the front door of his lodge where, this morning, we watch herring feed in the light of early dawn – scores of them jumping, so many they make the water look as if it is being rippled by a constant wind.

Bearing thermoses of coffee, we motor into an Emily Carr landscape. Low cloud drapes the shoreline, the labyrinthine inlets, and the lagoons and rocky coves where cedar and hemlock forests grow, it seems, out of stone. At least 100 seals loll on what locals call Ten Mile Point. A bald eagle, totem of the tribe that adopted Bejcar when he married a Nisga'a woman, circles and lands on a nearby rock. We drift in Crow Lagoon, 10 seals barking at us, half of them white. We meander from inlet to inlet for hours, idly scanning the waves for dorsal fins and the shoreline for signs of bears but seeing neither.

At Khutzeymateen Inlet, part of the protected territory of 40 to 60 grizzlies, park warden Norman Faithful, 42, tells us the bears have not been around the past few days, as they are following the salmon farther upstream. "But," he says, "even when you can't see them, you can feel their presence. It's a combination of freedom and power."

We carry on. I am lulled almost asleep by the rhythm of the boat, the quiet never-ending ocean, symbol of the subconscious, the unknown, and the ineffable. And then, in Work Channel, it happens. Bejcar stops the *Wilp Syoon 1*. I wake up fast.

Ten metres away the water is strangely flat and dark, forming an oval shape about the length of the boat. A ring of bubbles

Along the west coast of North America, most species of whales, including ones like this massive humpback, are rapidly recovering from 150 years of human predation. JOHN FORD/URSUS

surrounds the oval, and I have goose bumps on my arms. I am about to ask Bejcar what is going on when three humpback whales, each about 16 metres long and weighing nearly 40 tonnes, surface and breach, exposing their pinkish, fleshy throats and scalloped front flippers, slamming down on the water and splashing us. Immediately two of them come up *again* and dive, flicking their tails (one black, one white) as they swim away. But they surface *again,* playing, falling over one another, smacking their tails, and we cannot help but laugh. We follow these three for an hour. They come close enough for us to see the barnacles on their tails and to hear a faint yelping sound. They repeat their opening act, blowing air while swimming in a circle to trap herring in a curtain of bubbles, diving, tumbling onto one another. We are enthralled, speechless. ❀

MARINE MAMMALS: BREATHING SALT AIR

In the summer hundreds of wintering Steller's and California sea lions can be seen lolling about on Race Rocks, a small collection of islets at the south end of Vancouver Island. The rocks provide perfect "haul-outs" upon which the sea lions and seals are able to crawl. In early spring – February, March, and April – a few hundred sea lions hang around the log booms in front of the Harmac mill near Nanaimo chasing the herring that come there to spawn, and hundreds more visit Baynes Sound between Denman and Vancouver Islands. From June until September about 2,500 of the huge animals – males are up to three metres long and weigh a tonne, females are half that size – congregate at the breeding rookeries on the Scott Islands at the south end of the Queen Charlotte Islands. British Columbia's Triangle, Sartine, and Beresford Islands become home to about 800 pups every summer.

About 1,500 sea otters live year-round along the northwest coast of Vancouver Island, and the population is increasing by about 19 percent per year. Wiped out in the early part of this century, the sea otters have reestablished themselves following the release of 60 Alaskan otters near Kyuquot Sound during the late 1960s and early 1970s; there are now 300 in this area. Active and extremely playful, they have – as Vancouver Aquarium's John Ford says in a mock-boring, scientific voice – "a high cuddle coefficient." Translation? "They're cute little guys." As are seals, the most common being the 1.5-metre-long harbour seal. Seen everywhere along the coast, heads bobbing like kelp bulbs, diving and holding their breath for up to 20 minutes, and barking at intruders, they are kayakers' constant companions.

There are a few thousand Pacific white-sided dolphins on the B.C. coast, travelling year-round in schools of several hundred animals. These acrobatic creatures prefer the waters off Port Hardy, Bella Bella, and points north, including Haikai Provincial Recreational Area and Fitz Hugh Sound.

"B.C. is known as *the* place to see killer whales," says Ford. The 200 transient whales and 300 resident whales of Johnstone Strait, off northeast Vancouver Island, are attracted by the seals, salmon, and the region's "rubbing beaches," which have been created by the area's gravelly ocean floor. The resident whales are there from July to September to intercept migrating salmon; their whereabouts during the rest of the year is unknown. The transient whales, all of which have been individually identified and given such names as Sonora A 42, roam the continent's northern coast, eating warm-blooded creatures, including birds and marine mammals, but not fish. During July and August, the whales congregate at the mouth of the Tsitika River near Robson Bight, an ecological reserve.

Twenty thousand grey whales migrate from Baja, California, to Alaska from mid-March through May and are easily seen within two kilometres of the coastline, particularly between Ucluelet and Tofino on Vancouver Island. They are harder to see on their return to California in November and December because they are farther offshore and moving faster.

The place to see humpback whales is Langara Island in the northwest corner of the Queen Charlotte Islands. More than 100 humpbacks migrate to Hawaii in the winter and return in March or April. In fact, Langara Island also has populations of sea lions, killer whales, white-sided dolphins, grey whales, and fin whales, the second largest mammal on the planet.

OPPOSITE Reduced to a worldwide population of 20 in 1892, northern elephant seals, like this young male pup, now number 65,000. This baby will grow into a 6.5-metre-long adult, making it one of the world's largest aquatic carnivores. GRAHAM OSBORNE

And the sabbath rang slowly
In the pebbles of the holy streams.

– DYLAN THOMAS, "FERN HILL"

Beverley

A SECRET HOT SPRING NEAR KINCOLITH, BRITISH COLUMBIA. No one but Ken Bejcar, who works a 10-minute boat trip away, comes here. Perhaps some of the 500 Natives in nearby Kincolith know about it – a trapline undoubtedly came down this hill years ago – but Bejcar is the only one who actually makes the trek. No wonder. We have been scrambling over enormous deadfalls for half an hour. However, the thought of sitting in a natural hot spring surrounded by hemlocks and spruce is a pretty good lure after eight hours on the ocean in drizzle and fog. Good enough to have me bushwhacking through stinging nettle and thorny devil's club. Every so often Bejcar rewards me with a freshly picked huckleberry, sweet and juicy.

Finally he pulls a small shovel from where he has stashed it in a nearby tree and clears the fallen leaves off a 2.5-by-2-metre pool that looks just like any other pool that might form near a creek. The difference is, this one is *hot* (41 degrees Celsius) and filled with water that bubbles up from deep in the Earth – rainwater that fell perhaps 50 years ago and percolated down, heating up three degrees Celsius every 100 metres until, about two kilometres down, it boiled. Thankfully it comes up much more quickly than it went down – too quickly to cool off much, forced to the surface by hydraulic pressure, rich with the Earth's minerals.

Lying back in this deliciously hot water with my head resting on a boulder and my toes wriggling into the hot sand feels damn good. No wonder stories abound about the healing properties of the approximately 100 hot springs in Canada. Virtually all of them are located west of the Alberta foothills: differences in elevation provide the artesian-well effect, while lots of tectonic activity and its resulting fault lines produce perfect hot-spring plumbing systems and, in some places, hot rocks that are located relatively close to the surface. At the Meager Creek Hot Springs west of Pemberton, British Columbia, for example, a layer of 800-degree-Celsius rock – the remnant of a recent volcanic eruption – lies just a few kilometres below the surface.

A quick plunge into the cold water of the creek and I am quickly back in the hot pool, skin tingling, wondering what, besides me, would not be here if it were not for this hot spring. Its effect on the environment is not as obvious as is that of the

PREVIOUS PAGES Near the British Columbia-Yukon border, the Liard River Hotsprings, one of Canada's largest, fills pools with 43-degree-Celsius water. The warm steam heats the air and nearby soil, creating a micro-climate where southerly orchids, violets, and sundews thrive. GARY FIEGEHEN

Liard River Hotsprings. There, near the B.C.-Yukon border, the 43-degree-Celsius water changes everything, raising the air temperature to create frost-free soil. Two hundred and fifty species of boreal forest plants grow there, 14 because of the springs. There are exotic plants such as monkey flower, ostrich fern, lobelia, violets, and 14 species of orchids – all north of the Fifty-sixth parallel. And I remember the words of Gordon Soules, research scientist with the Geological Survey of Canada and author of *Hot Springs of Western Canada*: "Hot springs tend to get special ecosystems. They probably *all* have something special about them." ❈

I gently eased the throttle forward for the extra power required to lift the aircraft over 9,250-foot Stupendous Mountain. We would then cruise over green, placid Turner Lake and sideslip past spectac-ular Hunlen Falls, 1,300 feet of quicksilver that cascades into Lonesome Lake.

– RALPH EDWARDS, *RALPH EDWARDS OF LONESOME LAKE*

Daniel

APPROACHING HUNLEN FALLS, OUTSIDE NIMPO LAKE, BRITISH COLUMBIA. Con York, 61, shouts something incomprehensible over the de Havilland Beaver's drone and gestures out the plane's windscreen. Seven kilometres, straight ahead, mist rises around the distant water-fall like smoke above a smouldering candle. York began his avi-ation career in 1957, flying the same ancient plane he is piloting today. Flying is all he knows. Like the aircraft's greying, gold-toothed pilot, the plane, too, is a relic: the 48-year-old Beaver has seen more flying time (33,000 hours) than has any other of its make. York is certain the Beaver will outlast him.

York flies us through the column of mist above 260-metre-high Hunlen Falls, sideslips, pulls the floatplane's nose up, and set-tles onto remote Turner Lake, located high in British Columbia's mountainous Tweedsmuir Provincial Park east of Bella Coola. On this day the lake is full of trout and the sky is full of cumulus.

I approach the waterfall like an acolyte approaching a shrine: tentatively. Its presence in the spruce forest is first per-ceived – not so much *heard* as *felt* – as a low, guttural rumbling issuing from the chasm beneath my feet. I edge toward the falls' viewpoint, which is marked with signs that read: EXTREME DANGER. I ignore the signs, risking vertigo here above almost a

half kilometre of ether. The cataract is so huge – five times the height of Niagara Falls – that my eyes must scan downward along the perpendicular column, following great silver crescents of airborne water as they disintegrate into miasma. A rainbow arches above the foaming cauldron far, far below. As a child, I had read about Shangri-La and about Jimmy Angel's account of his discovery of Venezuela's Angel Falls. The entrance to paradise was marked, in my childhood mind, by a rainbow across the face of a great waterfall. The cynic in me suspects that today's children may envision the entrance as one marked by Golden Arches. ⊞

GREAT WATERFALLS

▸ DELLA FALLS, *at 440 metres the highest waterfall in North America, cascades over a very remote cliff northwest of Port Alberni, British Columbia.*

▸ TAKAKKAW FALLS, *254 metres high, is an impressive and easy-to-see cataract in British Columbia's Yoho National Park. Twin Falls, also in Yoho, is a matched set of cataracts, 82 metres high.*

▸ HELMCKEN FALLS, *in British Columbia's Wells Gray Provincial Park, is a spectacular sheer cascade that is 137 metres high.*

▸ PANTHER FALLS, *located south of Jasper, Alberta, drops 183 metres into a limestone canyon, just a short walk from the trailhead.*

Daniel

VULCANISM UP CLOSE IN THE RAINBOW RANGE WEST OF ANAHIM LAKE, BRITISH COLUMBIA. The 2,500-metre-high volcanic mountains of the Chilcotin Plateau emerge from the unusual midsummer snowfields as columnar basalt cliffs, eroded lava flows and, in the near distance, a series of ridgelines that grow more surreal as we approach. The ridges ahead, like the equally impressive Spectrum Range near British Columbia's northerly Mount Edziza, burn brilliantly with the colours of the land's igneous origins, the ancient magma and lava now sublimated into prismatic clays. These streak the ridge lines in iridescent oranges, bloody reds, chalky whites, mauves, ochres, sulphurous yellows: 200-metre-long talus slides of vibrancy. The strange colours are derived from the oxidation of the iron-rich basalt, ash, and lava that time,

"The plane's goin' strong. But I'm slowin' down," says 61-year-old bush pilot Con York as he sideslips his ancient Beaver floatplane above Hunlen Falls, one of the continent's highest cataracts. DANIEL WOOD

As the volcanic rocks oxidize
and break down, the yellows of
sulphur, the oranges and reds
of iron, and the creamy whites
of ash are released, creating
abstract flames that mimic the
original molten lava flows here.
DANIEL WOOD

heated ground water, rain, and air have transformed into tongues
of flaming earth. The ground seems to burn. As the airplane
banks steeply above the encircling ridges, it feels like we have
entered the vortex of a hellish cauldron and that we are plunging into molten metal. ▦

Beverley

**EATEN ALIVE BY MOSQUITOES EAST OF FIRVALE,
BRITISH COLUMBIA.** There are two black bears by the
side of the road. Watching them is like watching a
National Geographic special about bears: one ambles along, making quick work of a fallen rotten log with one scoop of his paw;
the other strolls ahead, pausing now and then to munch on a
clump of lupin.

The sign at the Ednarko River campsite in Tweedsmuir
Provincial Park warns us, in can't-miss-'em letters, that we are
camping in bear habitat – grizzly and black. I notice that when
Daniel goes to his tent for the night he takes his hatchet. This
does not reassure me.

I wake up in the middle of the night and start meandering
down the increasingly frightening mental path of wondering

what the bears are up to when I realize that my face is no longer my face but that of someone else. The stranger's forehead is lumpy, as though a dozen marbles have been inserted under her skin. Her right eye seems to be having trouble opening. Huge welts cover the right side of her neck. It seems that while I was worrying about bears I was kidnapped by aliens and returned after some serious medical experiments. This calls for some assistance. Recalling that hatchet, I try to make the scrambling from my tent to Daniel's as unbearlike as possible. "Something's happened to my head," I say. He fumbles around among zippers and pouches and shines his flashlight in my face. I can tell from the inside that it looks pretty bad from the outside. "I am *not* an animal," I say in my best Elephant Man voice.

"Ice," he says, and leaves.

The next thing I know he is handing me an apple. Great! An antidote for alien abduction I had never heard of before! But it is icy cold, from the cooler. Fortunately it is a red delicious apple with the little pointy bits on the end, which fit perfectly into the corner of my eye. So I lie there with fruit on my face for a while, hoping the swelling will go down. "It's the apple of my eye," I say, and laugh a bit more hysterically than the situation calls for.

In the morning Daniel points to a three-centimetre opening where I hadn't completely shut the back zipper of my tent. "Mosquitoes," he says, and offers to count the number of times they had claimed the right side of my head and neck as their prey while I had slept. Fifty-one, not counting the ones under my hair. He comforts me by telling me about the 100,000 types of venomous insects in the world, including a Costa Rican wasp that sprays venom into its enemy's eyes and the spider bite that dissolves its victim. I am humoured by these grotesqueries but not cured. He tells me the mosquito is honoured in Native myth and is depicted on totem poles. This information doesn't make me feel better, either. It strikes me as more than a little ironic that, here at the journey's end, after months of successfully defending myself against them, the mosquitoes have finally won. ✤

As the last words fall away,
the great and silent rivers of life
are flowing into the oceans,
and on a day like any other
they will carry you again,
abandoned,
on the currents you have fought,
to the place you did not know
you belonged.

– DAVID WHYTE, "CLOUD-HIDDEN"

Daniel

Over 100 enigmatic faces and figures stare outward from the granite bedrock and boulders above Thorsen Creek. No one knows where the images came from or what they mean. CHRIS HARRIS/FIRST LIGHT

THORSEN CREEK PETROGLYPHS, NEAR HAGENSBORG, BRITISH COLUMBIA. No one, not even 30-year-old Simon Fraser University archaeology student Brenda Gould, knows for certain what went on here. The story is lost in time. Beneath the hemlocks above flood-swollen Thorsen Creek, 14 kilometres east of Bella Coola, the boulders and ledges in the 1,500-square-metre site contain strange human figures, anthropomorphic beasts, geometric patterns, frogs, fish, and carved animal tracks – a collection of 111 images etched into the lichen-shrouded quartz-veined granite years, centuries, perhaps millennia ago. The bug-eyed, gape-mouthed heads remind me of Edvard Munch's dreamlike, expressionist work *The Scream*. The petroglyph site is, according to Gould, the richest source of prehistoric rock art in the Pacific Northwest.

These ochre pictographs, a few of the thousands at sites across southern British Columbia, are usually 20th-century creations. The hundreds of different stylized symbols are understood by Native elders, although the language of pictographs is now disappearing. GRAHAM OSBORNE

PETROGLYPHS AND PIC-TOGRAPHS: MYSTERIES IN GRANITE AND OCHRE

Unlike the early people of Latin America and the U.S. Southwest, the tribes of the Pacific Northwest built in wood, not stone. What remains of their sacred sites, with the exception of a very few surviving totem poles, are often only complex rock art hieroglyphics – graphic images inscribed on stone.

The most durable of these images are petroglyphs – rocks into which Natives have incised images. For example, two white quartzite boulders, located atop a grassy knoll near Kinsella, Alberta, are remnants of an ancient Cree ritual site. The rocks, called ribstones, depict the backbone and rib pattern of two buffalo. Archaeologists calculate that for 1,000 years the plains Indians utilized this hilltop location for sacrifices and offerings in order to ensure a successful buffalo hunt. It was only with the disappearance of the buffalo in the 1870s that the sacred stones fell into disuse. Elsewhere – at Writing-on-Stone Provincial Park in southern Alberta, on a roadside bluff outside Nanaimo, British Columbia, and at hundreds of other locations across the West – Natives left little more than graven images of their lives and spiritual world.

Tens of thousands of less durable pictographs, usually done in red and yellow ochre and drawn with a fingertip, dot rocky bluffs over much of south-central British Columbia. The southern Okanagan Valley, the Similkameen, and the Lillooet region are particularly important pictograph sites. The ochre – actually clays rich in reddish hematite and bright-yellow limonite – was collected at various well-established mines, such as the red cliffs near Tulameen, British Columbia, and Vermilion Springs in the Kootenay Mountains. First pulverized, then baked, then ground into a soluble powder, the refined colours were mixed with bear grease, fish eggs, fish oil, pitch, or even blood (it is rich in albumin) to ensure that they would bind. The colourful ores were then traded throughout the area and used for dyes, body painting, and the creation of rock paintings. The Natives drew upon a large repertoire of symbols to record their cliffside stories. Since the surviving pictographs are recent – almost all are of 20th-century application – scientists can draw on Native oral traditions to determine their meanings. Among the vast array of B.C. pictographs, there is no mistaking the humans, the deer, the fish, the sun, the moon, the bear prints, the rainbows, and the lightning bolts. The more anthropomorphic and abstract designs, however, are like half-remembered images in dreams, hinting at stories whose meanings are fading in the light of day.

She has spent six weeks here in the coastal rainforest, working with a transit, a tape measure, a variety of soft brushes, cameras, and an assistant who sketches the images onto graph paper, recording data and mapping the locale. She is calculating the age of the nearby trees, the speed of lichen growth on the granite surfaces, and the changes in design over time, hoping to better assess the age and meaning of the petroglyphs. She points to a large hemlock that has hollow-eyed faces staring upward from beneath its roots. The tree is at least 175 years old, so the rock art predates it. She shows me a strange figure, depicted as if in X-ray: all bones.

The unusual nature of the images here, quite different from the ovoids and rhomboids in other Northwest Coast art, leads archaeologists to suspect this was once a site for shamanic practices, where individuals came to submit to private trance-induced visions. If 19th-century ethnologists are correct, Gould tells me as we survey a set of faces set around a small waterfall, the surreal figures are part of some lost spiritual rites. "Important chiefs probably came here," she says. "To beat on the rocks, to practise keeping time, to practise their ceremonies and songs. A missed beat or an off-key note . . . it could be a disaster. The salmon might never come back if they sang off-key."

Yeah, I tell myself, the animistic mind is always looking for messages, implications, portents, meaning. I touch a face on the granite. It is fixed and cool. It is like my father's face before the nurse closed his eyes and mouth in his intensive-care bed: flesh become stone. ▨

If I take you to my island . . .
we'll lie on the sand
and feel the galaxy
on our cheeks . . .

– PAT LOWTHER, "SONG"

SAILING SOUTH ALONG FITZ HUGH SOUND NEAR NAMU, BRITISH COLUMBIA. Here at the frayed edge of North America the continent unravels into mist. Outside the ferry's windows, the blue-grey land merges into grey ocean and grey sky like a photograph emerging within a darkroom tray. Shades of shape; shades of meaning. Form is content. Behind us now stretches 32,000 kilometres of travel and ahead of us, 150 kilometres to the south, lies Port Hardy, our last destination, the place with the bizarre Shoe Tree where this long journey began. Beverley is curled up beside the window, recovering from the 51 mosquito bites, the jack-o'-lantern swelling of her face, and the soporific effect of heavy doses of antihistamine.

Along the ragged fjords and islands around us live the survivors of great Native maritime cultures whose worlds were overwhelmed in the past century or so. I know that there are still a few mouldering totem poles out there amid the salal, a few crypts and caves with the bones of the honoured dead, but the idea of their presence makes me feel sad for what has been lost. I know, too, that the coast we are passing contains the rotting timbers of many failed utopian dreams. Here, I tell myself, dreamers came, going westward as far as they could: to the continent's edge. Here dreams died. Behind us now lies Bella Coola where a group of Norwegians set up their utopia in 1894. The firs, the fjords, the greyness: it must have looked a lot like home to them. To our immediate right is storm-swept Hunter Island where Icelandic immigrants sought paradise but found instead cold and defeat. For a while, though, it also must have looked like home. Just ahead in the mist is Calvert Island, one of the thousands of islands and islets on the B.C. coast. Bead-wearing 1970s hippies established their utopian commune there, far from laws and civilization. Gone. All gone now. The coast is full of failed dreams. In fact, we have just left Ocean Falls where 30 years ago 2,500 people lived around a bustling pulp and paper mill. Today it is a virtual ghost town, full of empty houses and high-rises, standing silently, windowpanes intact, as though it had been abandoned in haste.

Islands are, by their nature, outposts of hope, and nature

ON THE PERIMETER OF THE DEEP   169

Blue-denim coastal islands, ridges in the mist, a cobalt sea, reflected sun-stars on the ocean, a breeze as soft as a lover's sigh, a tenting sun, a solitary gull – a day for metaphors, for thoughtlessness, for dreaming, for endings and beginnings. DANIEL WOOD

makes no allowances for hope. Nature simply *is*. Nature's and science's consolation is that, seen from a thoughtful perspective, both contain surprises. Sometimes these arrive, like a tornado or a circling red-tailed hawk, with the force of an omen and must be heeded. Sometimes they appear at the periphery of one's vision, like a moose cow and her calf, and then enter one's consciousness as epiphanies. Sometimes the surprises are there all along, like the flakes of worked basalt lying underfoot at a long-abandoned archaeological site or like a nighthawk's booming

courtship dive. All one has to do is look or listen. Sometimes, too, the surprises come in finding patterns, in discovering metaphors and analogies, in making connections between this and that. Off to our left, steep-sided Burke Channel opens to the east in ridge after plunging blue-grey ridge, each ending abruptly in the finality of water. The farther the ridge, the paler it appears. These cliffs go back and back, it seems, toward the continent's heartland, until the most distant fade into infinity and nothingness. ▦

BIBLIOGRAPHY

Alberta. Department of Forestry, Lands, and Wildlife. *Ecoregions and Ecodistricts of Alberta*. Edmonton, 1992.

——. ——. *Significant Natural Features of the Eastern Boreal Forest*. Edmonton, 1990.

——. Provincial Museum. *A Nature Guide to Alberta*. Edmonton: Hurtig, 1980.

Bailey, Ronald H. *Glacier*. New York: Time-Life, 1982.

Barry, P. F. *Mystical Themes in Milk River Rock Art*. Edmonton: U of Alberta P, 1991.

Belton, Peter. *The Mosquitoes of British Columbia*. Victoria: British Columbia Provincial Museum, 1983.

Bird, J. Brian. *Natural Landscapes of Canada*. Toronto: Wiley, 1972.

Brumley, John H. *Medicine Wheels on the Northern Plains*. Edmonton: Alberta Cultural and Multicultural, 1988.

Bryan, Liz. *British Columbia: This Favored Land*. Vancouver: Douglas and McIntyre, 1982.

——. *The Buffalo People: Prehistoric Archeology on the Canadian Plains*. Edmonton: U of Alberta P, 1991.

Bryan, Liz, and Jack Bryan. *Country Roads*. Vancouver: Sunflower, 1991.

Cannings, Richard, and Sydney Cannings. *British Columbia: A Natural History*. Vancouver: Greystone, 1996.

Carliss, William R. *Unknown Earth: A Handbook of Geological Enigmas*. Glen Arm, MD: Sourcebook Project, 1980.

Coull, Cheryl. *A Traveller's Guide to Aboriginal B.C.* Vancouver: Whitecap/Beautiful British Columbia, 1996.

Daley, Richard, and Chris Arnett. *They Write Their Dreams on the Rock Forever*. Vancouver: Talonbooks, 1993.

Davis, Richard A. *The Evolving Coast*. New York: Scientific American Library, 1994.

Environment Canada. *Marine Weather Hazards Along the British Columbia Coast*. Ottawa: Queen's Printer, 1987.

Fitzharris, Tim, and John Livingston. *Canada: A Natural History*. Markham, ON: Viking, 1988.

Fryer, Harold. *Stops of Interest in Central and Northern Alberta*. Surrey, BC: Heritage, 1982.

Gadd, Ben. *Handbook of the Canadian Rockies*. Jasper: Corax, 1995.

Gayton, Don. *Landscapes of the Interior*. Gabriola Island, BC: New Society, 1996.

——. *The Wheatgrass Mechanism : Science and Imagination in the Western Canadian Landscape*. Saskatoon: Fifth, 1990.

Gibbs, James. *Treasures of the Sea: Marine Life of the Pacific Northwest*. Toronto: Oxford UP, 1983.

Green, David M., and R. Wayne Campbell. *The Amphibians of B.C.* Victoria: Royal British Columbia Museum, 1984.

Grescoe, Paul, and Audrey Grescoe. *Fragments of Paradise: British Columbia's Wild and Wondrous Islands.* Vancouver: Raincoast, 1995.

Hardy, W. G., ed. *Alberta: A Natural History.* Edmonton: Patrons/Hurtig, 1967.

Hartmier, Richard. *Yukon: Colour of the Land.* Whitehorse: Lost Moose, 1995.

Heinl, Russ. *Where the Eagle Soars: Over British Columbia's Islands.* Vancouver: Raincoast, 1994.

Holland, Stuart S. *Landforms of British Columbia.* Victoria: Crown, 1976.

Institute of Arctic and Alpine Research. *Arctic and Alpine Research.* Boulder: U of Colorado, 1983.

Islands Protection Society. *Islands at the Edge.* Vancouver: Douglas and McIntyre, 1984.

Kramer, Pat. *Native Sites in Western Canada.* Banff: Altitude, 1994.

Kraulis, J. A. *Pacific Wilderness.* New York: Gallery, 1989.

Lawrence, R. D. *Canada's National Parks.* Toronto: Collins, 1983.

——. *A Natural History of Canada.* Toronto: Key Porter, 1988.

Lebowitz, Andrea Pinto, ed. *Living in Harmony: Nature Writing by Women in Canada.* Victoria: Orca, 1996.

Mackenzie, Ian. *Ancient Landscapes of British Columbia.* Edmonton: Lone Pine, 1996.

McConnaughey, Bayard, and Evelyn McConnaughey. *Pacific Coast.* New York: Knopf, 1985.

McGill, Bryan, ed. *Beautiful British Columbia Travel Guide.* Victoria: Beautiful British Columbia, 1994.

McLuhan, T. C. *Cathedrals of the Spirit.* Toronto: HarperCollins, 1996.

Milne, Courtney. *The Sacred Earth.* Toronto: Viking, 1991.

——. *Spirit of the Land.* Toronto: Viking, 1994.

Morris, Karin. *Petroglyphs of British Columbia.* Vancouver: Canadian Forest Products, 1972.

Neering, Rosemary. *British Columbia.* Vancouver: Whitecap, 1994.

Obee, Bruce, and Tim Fitzharris. *Coastal Wildlife of British Columbia.* Vancouver: Whitecap, 1991.

Patterson, Bruce. *Alberta Superguide.* Banff: Altitude, 1992.

Paulson, Dennis. *Shorebirds of the Pacific Northwest.* Vancouver: UBC Press, 1993.

Phillips, David. *The Climates of Canada.* Ottawa: Government Publication Centre, 1990.

Pratt-Johnson, Betty. *101 Dives.* Surrey, BC: Heritage, 1995.

Prest, V. K. *Canada's Heritage of Glacial Features.* Ottawa: Geological Survey of Canada, 1983.

Pringle, Heather. *In Search of Ancient North America*. New York: Wiley, 1996.

Rautio, Susanne, ed. *Community Action for Endangered Speciea*. Vancouver: Federation of British Columbia Naturalists, 1992.

Reeves, Brian O. K. *Head-Smashed-In: 5500 Years of Bison Jumping on the Alberta Plains*. Lincoln, NE: J and L Reprint, 1990.

Reimer, Phil. *B.C. Weather Book*. Vancouver: Phil Reimer Communications, 1991.

Rue, Walter. *Weather of the Pacific Coast*. Vancouver: Gordon Soules, 1978.

Russell, Andy. *Alpine Canada*. Edmonton: Hurtig, 1979.

Saling, Ann. *The Great Northwest Nature Factbook*. Anchorage: Alaska Northwest Books, 1991.

Savage, Candace. *Aurora: The Mysterious Northern Lights*. Vancouver: Douglas and McIntyre, 1994.

Schmidt, Dennis, and Esther Schmidt. *Western Wildlife*. Toronto: Oxford UP, 1983.

Scott, Shirley, ed. *Field Guide to Birds of North America*. Washington, D.C.: National Geographic Society, 1987.

Short, Steve, and Bernie Palmer. *Natural Highs*. Vancouver: Whitecap, 1992.

Spreitz, Karl. *Songs from the Wild*. Victoria: Beautiful British Columbia, 1992.

Stoltmann, Randy. *Hiking Guide to the Big Trees of Southwestern British Columbia*. Vancouver: Western Canada Wilderness Committee, 1987.

——. *Written by the Wind*. Victoria: Orca, 1993.

Suzuki, David. *Sciencescape: The Nature of Canada*. Toronto: Oxford UP, 1986.

Swan, James S. *Sacred Places*. Sante Fe: Bear, 1990.

Theberge, John B. *Kluane: Pinnacle of the Yukon*. Toronto: Doubleday, 1980.

Towriss, R. Wayne. *Yukon by Northern Light*. Whitehorse: Studio North, 1983.

van Everdingen, R. O. *Thermal and Mineral Hot Springs of the Southern Rocky Mountains of Canada*. Ottawa: Department of the Environment, 1972.

Wareham, Bill. *B.C. Wildlife Viewing Guide*. Edmonton: Lone Pine, 1991.

Woodward, Meredith, and Ron Woodward. *British Columbia Interior*. Banff: Altitude, 1993.

Yates, Steve. *Orcas, Eagles and Kings: The Natural History of Puget Sound and the Georgia Strait*. Boca Raton, FL: Primavera, 1992.

Young, Cameron. *The Forests of British Columbia*. Vancouver: Whitecap, 1985.

Zuehlke, Mark. *The B.C. Fact Book*. Vancouver: Whitecap, 1995.

INDEX

Page numbers referring to photographs and captions are in italics.